WORSHIP TIME with Kids

Bible-based Activities for Children's Church

WORSHIP TIME with Kids

Bible-based Activities for Children's Church

CINDY DINGWALL

Abingdon Press
Nashville

Worship Time with Kids
Bible-based Activities for Children's Church

Copyright © 1998 by Cindy Dingwall

This book is printed on recycled, acid-free, elemental-chlorine–free paper.

ISBN 0-687-05249-1

99 00 01 02 03 04 05 06 07—10 9 8 7 6 5 4 3 2

MANUFACTURED IN THE UNITED STATES OF AMERICA

To my trusted friend, Marjorie Janovics, who served as accompanist for our children's choir, God's Followers. Marge's joy and dedication as well as her love for all of us helped make our children's music program very special.

Contents

Acknowledgments

Many thanks to

Tom Ostrander, pastor of Church of the Incarnation for answering my myriad of questions and for all of the advice he provided with this book.

Louise Mahan, former pastor of Church of the Incarnation for encouraging me to make a big change in my life.

The late Jim Reid, former pastor of Church of the Incarnation for welcoming God's Followers gifts of music during our Sunday morning worship services.

Larry Hilkemann, former pastor of Church of the Incarnation for saying, "Sure you can!" when I wasn't at all sure I could present a children's sermon in church.

Diane Blizek, minister of music at Church of the Incarnation for teaching me how to conduct a choir and how to count music correctly.

Nancy Bavisotto for asking me to direct the children's Christmas musical in 1983. It was the beginning of our children's choir.

The children who were members of God's Followers from 1983–1989. You were a source of joy and inspiration in my life. Thanks to their parents for bringing them to rehearsals each week.

The members of Church of the Incarnation for welcoming my offerings of children's sermons, storytelling and other gifts . . . and of course for your prayers.

Abingdon Press for their support and encouragement.

The members of Lincoln Story League. Being a part of this storytelling group is a blessing.

The following libraries for providing outstanding facilities and resources: Arlington Heights Memorial Library, Barrington Area Library, Ela Area Library, Indian Trails Public Library, Mount Prospect Public Library, Palatine Area Public Library, and Prospect Heights Public Library.

All of my friends. I couldn't have done this without your prayers and encouragement.

Introduction

Worship Time with Kids is a cornucopia of ideas for sharing joyful and thoughtful worship experiences with children. Through these activities children will come closer to God and will recognize their special place in God's world.

Age recommendations are given throughout the book. Ideas marked Preschool and Kindergarten are intended for children from three to six years. Activities marked Elementary School are for children from 6 to 10 years or from first through fifth grade. However, feel free to be flexible when using material with children. If something for younger children works well with your elementary age group, use it, and vice versa.

You will find throughout the book puzzles, games, and activities that can be used to enhance children's worship. Several other ideas that can also be used are featured in my book *Bible Time with Kids* (see Resource List). Use these as worship activity sheets, in Children's Church, your Sunday church bulletin, the church newslettter, any place that children would enjoy them.

SOMETHING SPECIAL

Throughout this book you will find songs and stories that can be used to enhance your worship experiences.

The Resource List in the appendix provides ordering information for these materials.

Look for these icons throughout the book:

 Preschool and Kindergarten level activity

 Elementary school level activity

 Appropriate for all ages

 Something Special

 Song

 Variations

Now, gather the children and praise the Lord. As Jesus said, "Let the children come to me." Come to Jesus and bring the children!

HINTS FOR USING PUZZLES WITH CHILDREN

1. Since children have a variety of abilities, feel free to adapt puzzles for use with the children.
—Make puzzles more challenging by adding more lines.
—Make puzzles easier by removing lines.
—Have children work together on puzzles. Give one scrambled word to each child. Use easier words with young children and more difficult words with older children.
—Fill in some of the letters or words of puzzles.
—On coloring puzzles, outline the pictures or letters with the appropriate color. Let the child color it in.
—Do the puzzle as a group.

2. If a child dislikes doing puzzles, provide an alternative activity (drawing, listening to a book with a tape, or listening to a music cassette).

Part 1: WORSHIP IDEAS AND ACTIVITIES

The activities in this section allow children to worship God through speaking, music, and movement and include calls to worship, litanies, affirmations, prayers, and benedictions.

The spoken activities help children learn to speak to God and invite children to joyfully praise the Lord.

Singing is also a way of praising and glorifying God. It is a form of prayer and a way of reaching out to God. We can give thanks through our music. Music is an expression of our love for one another and the Lord. It allows us to share in God's messages of love, forgiveness, and acceptance and can be a way of learning about the lessons that are found in the Bible. Prayer allows us to talk to God at any time we choose.

Each of these activities, songs, and prayers will help children draw closer to God.

Chapter 1: Calls to Worship

The call to worship occurs at the beginning of the service. It opens the worship service, and it is an invitation that helps prepare us for worship. We can have a spoken or musical call to worship. Sometimes we have both.

Relate the call to worship to the "warm-ups" athletes do before they practice or play a game. Talk about the warm-ups singers do at the beginning of a choir rehearsal.

The spoken calls to worship presented here involve movement and repetition, while the musical calls to worship allow children to sing praises to our Lord.

Many of these calls to worship can also be used to open a children's choir rehearsal or start the day in parochial day care centers or elementary schools. A musical call to worship is sometimes referred to as an introit. The word *introit* means invitation. We are inviting people to join us as we worship God. It's another way to get us "warmed up" for church.

GOOD MORNING

 Scripture: Psalm 59:16

Leader: Good Morning!

Children: Good Morning!

Leader: I'm glad to see you!

Children: I'm glad to see you!

Leader: Let's jump up high and shout, "PRAISE GOD!"

Children: Let's jump up high and shout, "PRAISE GOD!"

Leader: Now let's all sit down. *(Leader sits)*

Children: Now let's all sit down. *(Kids sit)*

 ❀ Ideas ❀

Experiment with other movements you can use. (Example: Let's stamp our feet and shout, "PRAISE GOD!"

COME ON!

 Scripture: Psalm 34:11 (adapted)

Leader: Come on! Let's get ready! *(Make "come" motion.)*

Children: Come on! Let's get ready! *(Make "come" motion.)*

Leader: Let's get ready to learn about God's love. *(Point up)*

Children: Let's get ready to learn about God's love. *(Point up)*

Leader: God loves you *(Point to others)*!

Children: God loves you *(Point to others)*!

Leader: And God loves me *(Point to self)*!

Children: And God loves me *(Point to self)*!

Leader: God loves everyone we see!
(*Spread arms wide, point to self, point to eyes.)*

Children: God loves everyone we see!
(*Spread arms wide, point to self, point to eyes.)*

Leader: Hooray! HOORAY!! HOORAY!!!

Children: Hooray! HOORAY!! HOORAY!!! *(Each "hooray" is shouted louder. Jump up high on each "hooray.")*

REJOICE, GIVE THANKS, BE GLAD!

 Scripture: Psalm 118:24

Leader: This is the day that God has made.

Children: Let us rejoice in it!

Leader: Let us give thanks for it!

Children: Let us be glad in it!

Leader: REJOICE!

Children: REJOICE!

Leader: GIVE THANKS!

Children: GIVE THANKS!

Leader: BE GLAD!

Children: BE GLAD!

Leader: REJOICE, GIVE THANKS, BE GLAD!

Children: REJOICE, GIVE THANKS, BE GLAD!

❋ Ideas ❋

1. Follow this call to worship with the musical call to worship, "It's a New Day" on page 15.

2. Encourage the children to think of appropriate motions.

ART: A NEW DAY

 Scripture: Psalm 118:24

MATERIALS: White paper, crayons, glue sticks (optional), envelopes (optional)

DIRECTIONS

1. Let the children draw original pictures of a new day.

❋ Idea ❋

1. Use this with "Rejoice, Give Thanks, Be Glad" above, and "It's a New Day" on page 15.

2. Encourage older children to write stories to accompany their pictures, telling what they like best about new days.

 VARIATION

Find color photographs of morning scenes (include sunrise pictures). Cut them out. Give each child a piece of paper, an envelope of pictures, and a glue stick. Let the children make a collage.

ACTIVITY: LET'S JUST PRAISE THE LORD YOU'RE HERE!

 Scripture: Psalm 40:16

MATERIALS: One beanbag per group

DIRECTIONS

1. Divide children into small groups. You will need one adult per group.

2. Give each group a beanbag.

3. Have the children form a circle, with the adult standing in the center.

Leader: *(Tosses bag to child.)* Welcome (child's name)! Let's just praise the Lord you're here!

Child: *(Catches bag and tosses it back to leader.)* Great is the Lord!

4. Continue until all children have had a turn.

5. End with "GREAT IS THE LORD!"

LET'S PRAISE THE LORD

 Scripture: Psalm 150:3-4

MATERIALS: Rhythm instruments

Leader: Let's praise the Lord! Clap your hands and shout "Yeah, God!"

Children: *(Clap hands)* "Yeah, God!"

Leader: Stamp your feet and shout "Yeah, God!"

Children: *(Stamp feet)* "Yeah, God!"

Leader: Let's praise the Lord!

Children: Let's praise the Lord!

Leader: Praise God with the instruments!

Children: *(Children play the instruments.)*

Leader: Play them once again, please!

Children: *(Children play the instruments.)*

Leader: Let's praise the Lord!

Children: Let's praise the Lord!

✳ Ideas ✳

1. Encourage the children to think of creative ways of using the rhythm instruments, their hands, feet, and other body parts to make music.
2. Challenge older children by combining actions. (Stamp your feet and play the instruments.)
3. Begin with the musical call to worship, "Praise the Lord" on page 17 and follow it with this one.

IT'S A NEW DAY!

 Scripture: Psalm 118:24

 (Sung to "Frere Jacques")

It's a new day!

It's a new day!

Let's rejoice!

Let's rejoice!

Rejoice and be glad!

Rejoice and be glad!

In this day!

In this day!

To teach the above song, sing the first line to the children and have them sing it back to you. After a few times through they will know it, and you can sing the entire song together. This is called antiphonal singing.
Divide the children into two groups and sing antiphonally. Group 1 sings line 1, and group 2 sings the repeat. Older children can sing this as a round.

LET'S WORSHIP GOD

 Scripture: Psalm 66:1

 (Sung to "The Bear Went Over the Mountain")

Let's worship God, let's worship God, let's worship God

    with joyful hearts,

    with joyful hearts,

    with joyful hearts,

Let's worship God,

With joyful hearts!

✳ Idea ✳

Use with "We Love God" below.

GAME: WE LOVE GOD

 Scripture: Psalm 66:1

MATERIALS: A large heart cut from red construction paper, individual photos of each child (or each child's name written on a piece of paper), tape, blindfold (optional for preschool children)

PREPARATION

1. Tape the large heart to the wall at "child level."

2. Put a piece of rolled tape on the back of each photo/name.

DIRECTIONS

1. Blindfold one child.

2. Spin the child around three times.

3. Give the child his or her photo or name.

4. Pointing the child in the direction of the large heart, have the child place his or her photo/name inside the heart, and say, "I love you, God!"

5. Ask the other children to respond with, "God loves (child's name)." Repeat, until each person has a turn.

6. Use with the worship service "Love One Another" on page 163.

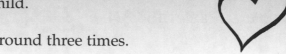

PRAISE THE LORD

 Scripture: Psalm 150:3-5

MATERIALS: Rhythm instruments

 (Sung to "Row, Row, Row Your Boat")

Praise, praise, praise the Lord;

Praise God joyfully.

Play your drums, clap your hands,

Praise God every day!

Praise, praise, praise the Lord;

Praise God joyfully.

Shake your bells, clap your hands,

Praise God every day!

Praise, praise, praise the Lord;

Praise God joyfully.

Praise, praise, praise the Lord;

Praise God joyfully.

Tap your sticks, clap your hands,

Praise God every day!

✳ Ideas ✳

1. Create verses for the instruments you use.

2. Use the instruments mentioned in the scripture.

3. Let the older children sing the song while the younger ones play the instruments.

4. Combine this song with "Let's Praise the Lord" on page 15. Begin with the spoken call to worship, followed by this one.

WELCOME

 Scripture: Matthew 25:35

 (Sung to "Frere Jacques")

Welcome _____ (Name)

Welcome _____ (Name)

To our class,

To our class.

We're glad you've come to join us.

We're glad you've come to join us.

Be our friend.

Be our friend.

✳ Hint ✳

This is a nice way to welcome new or visiting children to your class or group. You can also use the song to welcome each child to the day's activity.

✳ Ideas ✳

1. Give each new or visiting child a small gift (pencil or magnet with your church name printed on it).

2. Give each new or visiting child the "Welcome!" puzzle on page 18.

3. Give the child's parent(s) information about your children's ministry program.

PUZZLE: WELCOME!

We are glad you came to worship with us this morning. We hope you come again.

Color: B: Blue R: Red
P: Purple K: Pink
G: Green O: Orange
Y: Yellow L: Lavender

IF YOU WANT TO PRAISE GOD

 Scripture: Psalm 47:1

 (Sung to "If You're Happy")

If you want to praise God, clap your hands
(clap, clap).

If you want to praise God, clap your hands
(clap, clap).

If you want to praise God,

If you want to praise God,

If you want to praise God, clap your hands
(clap, clap).

Other verses: Stamp your feet.
Click your tongue.
Shout "I love you!"

✳ Idea ✳
Let the children think of other verses.

COME TO CHRIST'S TABLE

 Scripture: Matthew 26:26-27

Leader: Come to Christ's table.
Children: We will come with love in our hearts.
Leader: Come and share a meal.
Children: We will come and ask for God's forgiveness.
Leader: Come and eat the bread.
Children: For it is Christ's body.
Leader: Come drink from the cup.
Children: For it is Christ's blood shed for me.
Leader: Come to God's table.
Children: We will come with love in our hearts.

✳ Idea ✳
Combine this with "We'll Remember Christ's Love" on page 21.

PUZZLE: WORSHIPING GOD

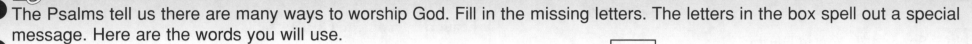

The Psalms tell us there are many ways to worship God. Fill in the missing letters. The letters in the box spell out a special message. Here are the words you will use.

Clap Hands   Shouting

Gladness   Joyfully

Instruments   Thanksgiving

Singing   Dancing

Rejoice

```
_ L _ _ _  H A _ _ D S

_ N _ T _ U _ E _ T _

     D _ N C _ N _

_ H A _ K S G _ V _ N G

   _ _ H O _ _ I N _

    R _ _ J O I _ _ E


   _ _ I N _ _ I _ G

      J _ _ Y F _ _ L L _

   G _ _ A _ _ N _ S S
```

WE'LL REMEMBER CHRIST'S LOVE

Scripture: Luke 22:14-20

(Sung to "Michael Row the Boat Ashore")

We will break this bread together, Alleluia.

We will break this bread together, Alleluia.

We will drink this juice (wine) together, Alleluia.

We will drink this juice (wine) together, Alleluia.

We'll give thanks to Christ who died, Alleluia.

We'll give thanks to Christ who died, Alleluia.

Jesus died to save us all, Alleluia.

Jesus died to save us all, Alleluia.

We'll remember Christ's love, Alleluia.

We'll remember Christ's love, Alleluia.

☀ Ideas ☀

1. Combine this call to worship with others on page 19.

2. Invite the children or your children's choir to sing this for a communion service.

3. "Worship Talks for Holy Communion" are on page 128.

BLESS THIS MEAL

Scripture: Matthew 26:26-27

(Sung to "Mary Had a Little Lamb")

Bless this meal that we share, that we share,
   that we share.

Bless this meal that we share,
   that we share together.

Bless this bread that we eat, that we eat,
   that we eat.

Bless this bread that we eat, that we eat
   together.

Bless this juice (wine) that we drink, that we drink,
   that we drink

Bless this juice (wine) that we drink, that we drink
   together.

Remember that Christ died for us, died for us,
   died for us.

Remember that Christ died for us,
   to save us from our sins.

HOSANNA! BLESSED IS HE WHO COMES!

 Scripture: Mark 11:9

Leader:	Hosanna!
Children:	Hosanna in the highest!
Leader:	Blessed is he who comes
Children:	In the name of the Lord!
Leader:	Hosanna!
Children:	Hosanna in the highest!

Have the children raise their arms up high overhead and wave their palms as they shout "HOSANNA IN THE HIGHEST!"

✳ Ideas ✳

1. Combine this with "Hosanna" below.

2. See page 129 for a worship talk about Palm Sunday.

HOSANNA

 Scripture: Matthew 21:6-9

 (Sung to "Frere Jacques")

Hosanna! Hosanna!

Here comes Jesus! Here comes Jesus!

Riding on a donkey! Riding on a donkey!

Wave your palms! Wave your palms!

Hosanna! Hosanna!

In the highest! In the highest!

Blessed is Jesus! Blessed is Jesus!

Who comes in the name

Of the Lord!

✳ Ideas ✳

1. This song can be sung antiphonally or as a round.

2. Let the children sing this song as they enter the sanctuary carrying palm branches on Palm Sunday.

3. Invite the congregation to join the children as they sing this song. The children can sing the first line, and the congregation can sing the repeat.

4. Older children can sing this as a round.

5. Combine this with the spoken call to worship, "Hosanna! Blessed Is He Who Comes!"

GOOD NEWS!

 Scripture: Matthew 28, Mark 16, Luke 24:1-49, John 20–21. Read or tell the Easter story to the children.

Leader: Jesus is risen!

Children: Good news!

Leader: Jesus lives!

Children: Good news!

Leader: Alleluia!

Children: Alleluia!

> ✳ **Idea** ✳
>
> Combine this with "It is Easter!" on page 24.

DID YOU HEAR WHAT HAPPENED?

 Scripture: Matthew 28, Mark 16, Luke 24:1-49, John 20–21

Leader: Did you hear what happened?

Children: What happened?

Leader: The women went to the tomb to anoint Jesus.

Children: What happened?

Leader: Jesus wasn't there!

Children: What happened?

Leader: Jesus had risen from the dead!

Children: AWESOME!

> ✳ **Idea** ✳
>
> Combine this with the musical call to worship "Have You Heard?" on page 24.

> ✳ **Hint** ✳
>
> Explain that Jewish custom required that the body of a dead person be anointed with oil. Mary and the other women went to the tomb on Sunday morning to anoint Jesus' body. The women brought pleasant smelling spices and oils to the tomb to show their love and respect for Jesus. We show love and respect for our loved ones when we bring flowers to their graves.

IT IS EASTER

Scripture: Matthew 28, Mark 16, Luke 24:1-49, John 20-21

(Sung to "Frere Jacques")

It is Easter!

It is Easter!

Christ is risen!

Christ is risen!

Sing a song of praise!

Sing a song of praise!

Alleluia!

Alleluia!

☀ Ideas ☀

1. This can be sung antiphonally or as a round.

2. Have a basket of flower petals. Let the children scatter flower petals on the floor as they sing. Use with the Easter Worship Talk on page 130, or Easter prayers are on pages 74-75.

HAVE YOU HEARD?

Scripture: Matthew 28, Mark 16, Luke 24:1-49, John 20-21.

(Sung to "Did You Ever See a Lassie?")

Have you heard the good news, the good news,

the good news?

Have you heard the good news about

Jesus Christ?

For Christ has risen!

And Christ is living!

And that is the good news about

Jesus Christ!

☀ Ideas ☀

1. Sing this after "Did You Hear What Happened?" on page 23.

2. See page 100 for Easter Benedictions.

ACTIVITY: COME, GIVE THANKS

 Scripture: Psalm 105:1

MATERIALS: Masking tape

PREPARATION
Use the tape to make a circle on the floor.

DIRECTIONS
1. Have the children stand around the circle.

2. As you call out each child's name, that child joins you inside the circle.

Leader: (Child's Name), come give thanks to the Lord

Child: *(Comes into circle)* Thank you God.

Leader: (Child's Name), come give thanks to the Lord

Child: *(Comes into circle)* Thank you God.

Invite the children to enter the circle in a variety of ways: jump, hop, crawl, skip, roll.

GIVE THANKS TO GOD

Scripture: Psalm 100:4

MATERIALS: a beanbag, masking tape

PREPARATION
Use the tape to make a circle on the floor.

DIRECTIONS
1. Have the children scatter themselves around the outside of the circle.

2. Standing in the middle of the circle, the leader tosses the beanbag to a child and says: "(Child's Name), enter God's gates with Thanksgiving!"

3. The child catches the beanbag, enters the circle and says, "I enter God's courts with praise!"

4. That child tosses the beanbag to another child and they repeat the exchange.

5. When all the children are inside the circle everyone says: "Give thanks to God, bless God's name."

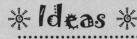

☀ Ideas ☀

1. Combine this with the musical call to worship "Enter God's Gates with Thanksgiving" on page 26.

2. Use with "We Are Thankful" on page 27.

3. See the theme index for other Thanksgiving worship ideas.

4. Use with worship service "Give Thanks and Share" page 158.

COME, SAY THANK YOU

Scripture: Psalm 105:1

(Sung to "Frere Jacques")

Come say thank you.

Come say thank you.

Thanks be to God!

Thanks be to God!

God gives us many blessings.

God gives us many blessings.

We love God.

We love God.

☀ Ideas ☀

1. Combine this with "Come Give Thanks" on page 25. Begin with the spoken call to worship. When all of the children are inside the circle, sing the song.
2. Sing this antiphonally or as a round.
3. Use with the "We Are Thankful" puzzle on page 27.
4. Try the Thanksgiving Prayers on page 74.

ENTER GOD'S GATES WITH THANKSGIVING

Scripture: Psalm 100:4

(Sung to "Here We Go Round the Mulberry Bush")

Enter God's gates with thanksgiving, thanksgiving,

thanksgiving.

Enter God's gates with thanksgiving

And come into God's courts with praise!

Give thanks to God and bless his name, bless his name, bless his name.

Give thanks to God and bless his name

And come into his courts with praise!

☀ Ideas ☀

1. Combine this with "Give Thanks to God" on page 25. Begin with the spoken call. When all the children are inside the circle sing the song.
2. A Thanksgiving worship service appears on page 158.

ART: I'M THANKFUL FOR

MATERIALS: 1 brown cut-out of a large cornucopia for each child, glue sticks, pictures of things we are thankful for, envelopes

DIRECTIONS

1. Give each child a cornucopia and an envelope filled with pictures of things we are thankful for.

2. Have the children glue the pictures to their cornucopias.

PUZZLE: WE ARE THANKFUL

Unscramble these words to find things we are thankful for, and print them in the spaces. Write the circled letter in each word in the space at the left.

When you finish the puzzle, draw pictures of things you are thankful for.

___ THCLOES   __ __ __ Ⓞ __ __ __

___ RUCHCH   __ Ⓞ __ __ __ __

___ MALSANI   Ⓞ __ __ __ __ __ __

___ SDNEIRF   __ __ __ __ Ⓞ __ __

___ KOOBS   __ __ __ Ⓞ __

___ MAFLIY   __ __ __ __ Ⓞ __

___ MEHO   __ Ⓞ __ __

___ SELFYOUR   __ __ Ⓞ __ __ __ __ __

___ DOG   Ⓞ __ __

___ TSOY   __ Ⓞ __ __

___ DOOF   __ __ Ⓞ __

LET'S GET READY

 Scripture: Isaiah 7:14

Leader: Let's get ready!

Children: Let's get ready!

Leader: Let's get ready for Baby Jesus!

Children: Let's get ready for Baby Jesus!

Leader: Only four more weeks till his birthday!

Children: Only four more weeks till his birthday!

Leader: Let's light the Advent wreath!

Light the appropriate candle on the Advent wreath.

> ## ❄ Hint ❄
>
> Each week the third line will change. (example: "Only three more weeks till his birthday.")

JESUS IS A COMIN'

 Scripture: Numbers 24:17

All: Jesus is a comin', a comin', a comin'!
Jesus is a comin', in four more weeks!
He's comin' to bring glory and salvation to the world!
He's comin' to bring glory and salvation to the world!
Gotta get ready to welcome Jesus Christ!
Gotta get ready to welcome Jesus Christ!

> ## ❄ Ideas ❄
>
> 1. Combine this with the call to worship "Time to Light the Advent Wreath" on page 29. Do this first, followed by the song.
>
> 2. See pages 134-38.

> ## ❄ Hints ❄
>
> 1. Do this as a rap. As you say it alternate clapping hands and snapping fingers to go with the rhythm. (example: Clap on Jesus; snap on *is a;* clap on *com;* snap on *in;* clap on *four;* snap on *more;* clap on *weeks!* Once you get the clapping and snapping going it really does come quite naturally.
>
> 2. Each week change line 2 to coincide with the number of weeks left until Christmas.
>
> 3. On Christmas Eve use "Welcome the King" page 30.

TIME TO LIGHT THE ADVENT WREATH

 Scripture: Isaiah 7:14

 (Sung to "Mary Had a Little Lamb")

Time to light the Advent wreath, Advent wreath,
   Advent wreath.
Time to light the Advent wreath,
Preparing for Christ's birthday.

❋ Hint ❋

Sing this refrain each week. Add the appropriate verse.

The first candle is one of promise,
   one of promise, one of promise.
The first candle is one of promise,
The promise Christ brought to us.

The second candle is one of hope,
   is one of hope, is one of hope.
The second candle is one of hope,
The hope Christ brought to us.

The third candle is one of peace,
   one of peace, one of peace.
The third candle is one of peace,
The peace Christ brought to us.

The fourth candle is one of joy,
   one of joy, one of joy.
The fourth candle is one of joy,
The joy Christ brought to us.

❋ Ideas ❋

1. Combine this with "Let's Get Ready" on page 28. Sing this song after the spoken call to worship.

2. The Christmas Eve portion of this song is found on page 31.

3. Invite a different child to light the Advent wreath each day or week.

4. See pages 159-61 for "Prepare the Way of the Lord."

TIME TO GET READY

  Scripture: Luke 2:10

Leader: Time to get ready!

Children: Time to get ready!

Leader: To celebrate a birthday!

Children: To celebrate a birthday!

Leader: It is Jesus' birthday!

Children: It is Jesus' birthday!

Leader: Happy birthday, Jesus!

Children: Happy birthday, Jesus!

> ### ❋ Ideas ❋
>
> 1. Combine this with the musical call to worship, "Lighting the Christ Candle" on page 31.
>
> 2. There are worship talks on pages 134-37
>
> NOTE: This is a spoken antiphon.

WELCOME THE KING

 Scripture: Luke 2:10

Jesus Christ was born one night!

Over Bethlehem shined the brightest light!

The angels were singin' with all of their might!

To welcome the King who was born that night!

> ### ❋ Ideas ❋
>
> 1. Combine this with "Born in Bethlehem" on page 32.
>
> 2. See pages 137-38 for a special Christmas eve worship talk.
>
> 3. Try the litany on page 50, or prayers on pages 78-79.
>
> 4. This is the final verse to "Jesus Is a Comin'" on page 28. Do it as a rap.

LIGHTING THE CHRIST CANDLE

 Scripture: Isaiah 9:6

 (Sung to "Mary Had a Little Lamb")

This is the night of Jesus' birth,

Jesus' birth, Jesus' birth.

This is the night of Jesus' birth.

We'll celebrate together.

We'll light the Christ candle on

the Advent wreath, Advent wreath, Advent wreath

We'll light the Christ candle on the Advent wreath.

It's the candle of love.

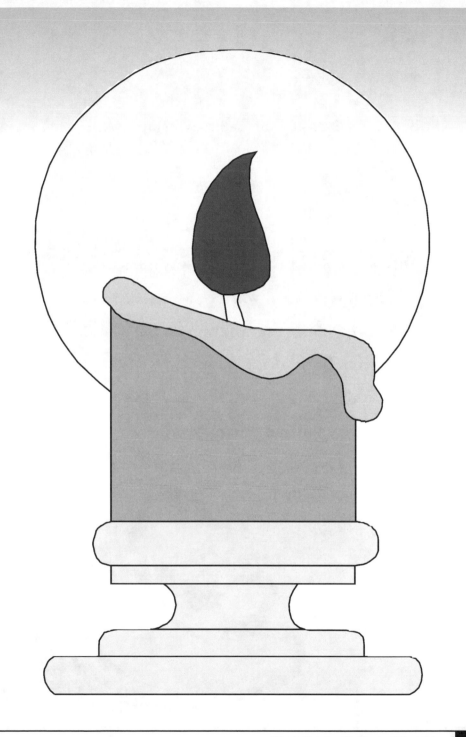

BORN IN BETHLEHEM

Scripture: Luke 2:7

On Christmas Eve, sing this call to worship.

(Sung to "Wheels on the Bus")

This is the night that Christ was born,

Christ was born, Christ was born.

This is the night that Christ was born,

Born in Bethlehem.

The white candle is one of love,

one of love, one of love.

The white candle is

one of love,

For the

love of

Christ.

LOOK WHO'S COMING TO VISIT JESUS

Scripture: Matthew 2:7-11

Leader: Look who's coming to visit Jesus!

Children: Look who's coming to visit Jesus!

Leader: The Wise Men are coming to visit Jesus!

Children: The Wise Men are coming to visit Jesus!

Leader: They are bringing gifts to baby Jesus!

Children: They are bringing gifts to baby Jesus!

Leader: They are bringing gold, frank-incense, and myrrh!

Children: They are bringing gold, frank-incense, and myrrh!

☀ Ideas ☀

1. Have the children mimic "looking" motions: pointing to distance, making binoculars over eyes with hands, hand shielding eyes from sun as they look, and so forth.

2. Combine this with "The Wise Men" on page 33.

3. Dramatize this call to worship.

LOOK WHO'S A COMIN'!

Scripture: Matthew 2:7-11

All: Look who's a comin' to visit Jesus!

The Wise Men are comin' to visit

Jesus!

And they're a ridin' on camel back!

I wonder what they've got inside the sack!

They followed the brightest, shining star!

And they've all traveled from lands afar!

They've arrived at the house where Jesus lives.

I wonder what it is they're about to give!

Gold, frankincense, and myrrh are what they brought.

To the king that they all eagerly sought.

☀ Ideas ☀

1. Combine this with "The Wise Men."

2. Use the clapping hands/snapping fingers rhythm that you used with "Jesus Is a Comin'" on page 28. Alternate clapping and snapping on each major beat of the rhythm. Think of other movements to use.

3. Let the children dramatize this call to worship. Find an electric Christmas star. Hang it over the house where Jesus lives.

THE WISE MEN

Scripture: Matthew 2:7-11

(Sung to "Three Blind Mice")

The Wise Men

The Wise Men

See how they come.

See how they come.

They followed a

   star to Bethlehem,

Bringing gold,

   frankincense, and

   myrrh with them.

They wanted to

   honor the new

   born King.

The Wise Men

The Wise Men

☀ Ideas ☀

1. Combine this with "Look Who's Coming to Visit Jesus".

2. See "What Did They Wear?" on page 35.

3. Have several boys dress up as the Wise Men and make a surprise visit during the song. Let them tell about the gifts they bring and why they chose those gifts. When the wise men appear say: "Look who's here. It's the Wise Men!"

PUZZLE: WHAT DID THEY BRING?

 The Wise Men brought three gifts to Jesus. Unscramble the words to find out what they brought. Print the letters in the spaces provided.

DOLG ___ (○) ___ (○)

ESNECNIKNARF ___ (○) ___ ___ ___ ___ ___ ___ (○) ___ ___ ___

RHRYM ___ ___ ___ ___ (○)

Print the circled letters here. _____

Unscramble them and print them in these spaces.

____ ____ ____ ____ ____

Who was this person?

_____

Draw and color a picture of one of these things.

—The Wise Men looking for Jesus

—The Wise Men visiting Jesus

—The gifts the Wise Men gave to Jesus

PUZZLE: WHAT DID THEY WEAR?

Connect the dots to find out what the Wise Men wore on their heads. Color your picture.

• 4

• 2   • 6

• 3   • 5

• 1   • 7

Chapter 2: Litanies and Affirmations

A litany is a series of thoughts and comments which are joined together by a group response. The response can remain the same, or it can be different. The litanies presented here encourage lots of active participation from the children. In addition to ideas outlined in each activity, another way to include the children is to alternate the leader role. Divide your group by gender, with girls reading the leader part and boys reading the children part, or by age with older kids leading and younger kids responding. Or simply divide everyone into two groups. Group 1 leads while group 2 responds.

Affirmations help children to express their Christian beliefs. An affirmation is a statement that tells what we believe about God and Jesus.

Scripture suggestions are provided for each litany and affirmation. However, other verses can be substituted to fit your needs.

In this section you will also find several puzzles, games, and activities that will reinforce what the children will learn about God and Jesus.

WHO LOVES US?

 Scripture: Psalm 63:4

MATERIALS: 1 large picture of Jesus per child (use a variety of pictures: Jesus walking on water, healing the sick, calming the storm, and so forth), 1 sheet of colored construction paper per child, Contact paper, glue, masking tape

PREPARATION
1. Glue each picture to a piece of construction paper.

2. Cover pictures with Contact paper.

3. Use the tape to make a line on the floor.

DIRECTIONS
1. Have the children stand on the line, holding their pictures of Jesus face down.
2. Face the children with your picture held face down also.

Leader:	Who was born in Bethlehem?
Children:	Jesus! (*pictures up, then back down*)
Leader:	Who is God's son?
Children:	Jesus! (*pictures up, then back down*)
Leader:	Who loves the children?
Children:	Jesus! (*pictures up, then back down*)
Leader:	Who is our savior?
Children:	Jesus! (*pictures up, then back down*)
Leader:	Who loves us all very much?
Children:	Jesus! (*pictures up, then back down*)

 **※ Hint ※**

Coloring books are a good source of pictures. Purchase several copies and color each picture.

ART: JESUS LOVES ME

MATERIALS: 1 heart cut from pink paper for each child, 1 photo of each child (optional), 1 small picture of Jesus per child (Stickers work well.), red glitter, red yarn, paper hole punch, red marker, glue

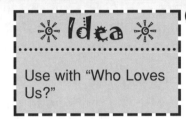
※ Idea ※

Use with "Who Loves Us?"

PREPARATION
1. Punch a hole in each heart. String a piece of red yarn through each heart and tie it in a loop.

2. Print *Jesus* on one side of the heart. On the other side print *loves* (child's name).

DIRECTIONS
1. Give each child a heart to decorate with red glitter.

2. Give each child a picture of Jesus. Have children glue the picture above the name *Jesus*.

3. Give each child their photo. Have children glue their photo above their name on the back of the heart.

4. Hang the hearts from the ceiling.

JESUS

Scripture: Matthew 1:21

MATERIALS: Colorful, wide-tipped markers, crayons, white paper (8" x 11"), cardboard, clear Contact paper, glue sticks, masking tape

PREPARATION

1. Use the markers to write each letter of *JESUS* on a piece of white paper (one letter per page).

2. Let the children use crayons to decorate the letters. Encourage the children to make them bright and colorful.

3. Cut out the letters and glue them to the cardboard.

4. Cover them with clear Contact paper.

5. Use the tape to make a line on the floor.

DIRECTIONS

1. Choose five children to hold the letters.

2. Give each child a letter, and have them stand in the proper order on the line, facing the other children. These children are called "Spirit Leaders."

3. The children sitting on the floor are called "Spirit Kids."

❋ Hint ❋

Each time you do this litany, choose different children to be "spirit leaders."

Leader 1:	Give us a J!
	(Jumps out, holds up letter)
Kids:	J *(shout)*
Leader 2:	Give us an E!
	(Jumps out, holds up letter)
Kids:	E *(shout)*
Leader 3:	Give us an S!
	(Jumps out, holds up letter)
Kids:	S *(shout)*
Leader 4:	Give us a U!
	(Jumps out, holds up letter)
Kids:	U *(shout)*
Leader 5:	Give us an S!
	(Jumps out, holds up letter)
Kids:	S *(shout)*
Leaders:	What does it spell?
Kids:	JESUS!
Leaders:	What does it spell:
Kids:	JESUS!
Leaders:	Who is Jesus?
Kids:	Jesus is God's son!
Leaders:	What did Jesus do?
Kids:	He died to save us from our sins.
Leaders:	Who do we love?
Kids:	JESUS!
Leaders:	Who do we love?
Kids:	JESUS!
Leaders:	And who loves us?
Kids:	JESUS!
All:	YES! JESUS!

PUZZLE: WHO IS JESUS?

Unscramble each word and print the letters in the blank spaces. In each line one letter is circled. Print that letter in the space to the left. When you are finished you will find another word for Jesus.

___ SUSEJ ___ ___ ◯ ___ ___

___ RACES ___ ◯ ___ ___ ___

___ OVEL ___ ___ ◯ ___

___ ENDFRI ___ ___ ◯ ___ ___ ___

___ IONNAPMOC ___ ___ ___ ___ ___ ___ ◯ ___

___ PERLEH ___ ___ ___ ___ ◯ ___

WHO DID THIS?

Scripture: Luke 4:14-15

MATERIALS: The *J E S U S* cards from the litany on page 38 and the Jesus pictures from the litany on page 37.

DIRECTIONS

1. Give the *J E S U S* cards to five children.

2. Give the Jesus pictures to the other children.

3. Intersperse the children with the *J E S U S* cards among the children holding the pictures.

4. Have the children sit or stand in a circle.

Leader: Who was the baby born in Bethlehem?

Children: Jesus was the baby born in Bethlehem.
(Hold up picture of Jesus in manger.)

Children: [with *J E S U S* cards] J-E-S-U-S
*(One at a time hold up card,
shout out letter.)*

Leader: Who taught the people how to pray?

Children: Jesus taught the people how to pray.
(Hold up picture of Jesus walking on water.)

☀ Hint ☀

The pictures should highlight the things you mention Jesus doing in the litany.

Children: [with *J E S U S* cards] J-E-S-U-S
(One at a time, hold up card and shout out letter.)

The leader will continue to ask questions. The children will respond using the pattern above.

☀ Idea ☀

Alternate older and younger children as the leader.

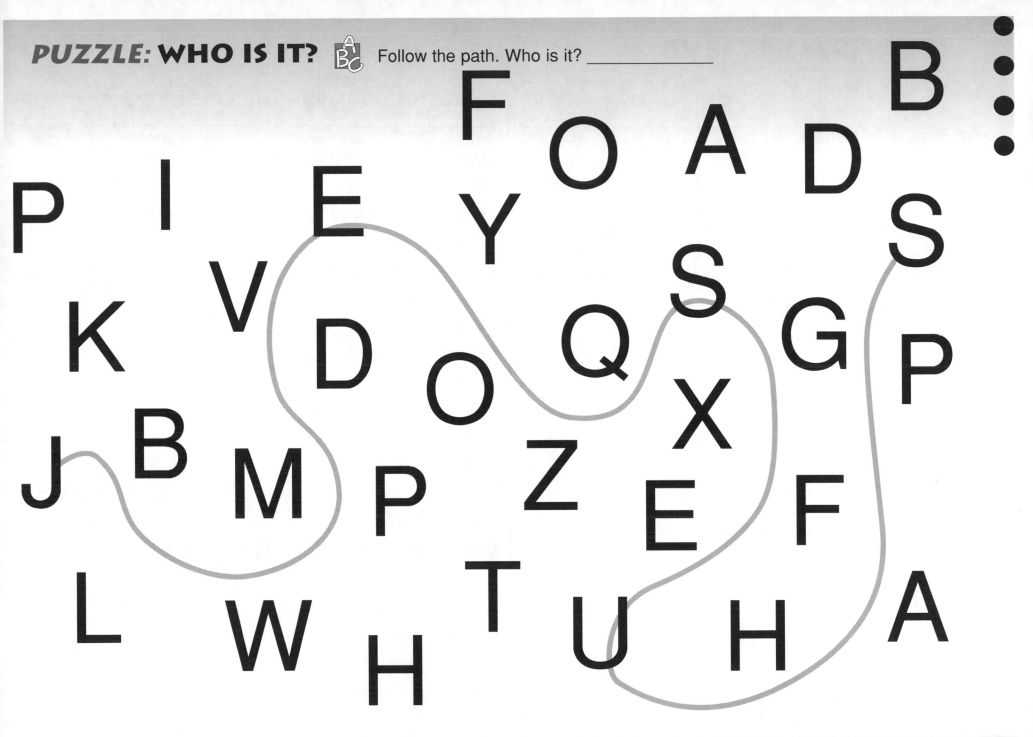

JESUS IS MY FRIEND

Scripture: John 15:14

(Sung to "Skip to My Lou")

Jesus Christ is my friend.

Jesus Christ is my friend.

Jesus Christ is my friend.

He is your friend too!

✻ Ideas ✻

1. Think of other verses to add to this litany. (Helper, Savior, other)

2. Encourage the children to think of appropriate motions.

WHO CREATED?

Scripture: Genesis 1:1–2:3

Tell the story of Creation to the children.

MATERIALS: Pictures of things God created, colored construction paper, clear Contact paper, glue

PREPARATION
1. Glue the pictures to construction paper.

2. Cover them with Contact paper.

DIRECTIONS
1. Sit or stand in a circle with the children.

2. As you ask each question, hold up the appropriate picture.

Leader: Who created night and day?

Children: God!

Leader: Who created sky and water?

Children: God!

Leader: Who created the earth?

Children: God!

Leader: Who created the sun, moon, and stars?

Children: God!

Leader: Who created birds and fish?

Children: God!

Leader: Who created animals and people!

Children: God!

Leader: Who said, "This is good!"

Children: God!

Leader: Who rested after creating the world?

Children: God!

Leader: Yeah, God!

Children: Yeah, God!

✻ Idea ✻

Make flannel board pieces for each item in the litany. Let the children take turns putting them on the flannel board as you say the litany.

THE BIG 10

Scripture: Exodus 20:1-17(adapted)

MATERIALS: 10 pieces of white paper, 10 pieces of colored poster board, colored markers with thick tips, glue sticks, clear Contact paper, masking tape

PREPARATION

1. Use colored markers to print one commandment on each piece of white paper. Use simple phrases and wording that are easy for children to understand and remember.

2. Glue each commandment to a piece of colored posterboard.

3. Print the words *THE BIG TEN* on the last piece of poster board.

4. Cover each piece of poster board with Contact paper.

5. Put a line of tape on the floor.

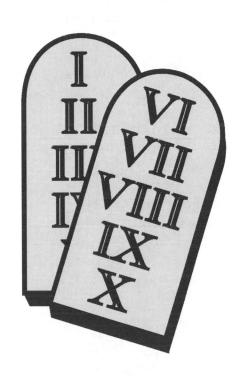

✳ Hint ✳

If you have a small group, give each child more than one commandment.

DIRECTIONS

1. Choose ten children. Give each person a commandment. Tell them to stand in various locations in the room. Have each child jump out when it is time for his or her commandment.

2. Ask another child to hold the card that says, THE BIG TEN. Have that child stand beside you.

3. Have the rest of the children sit on the floor in a group.

Child (with Big Ten):   Hey, everyone! It's the Big Ten!

Children: What?

Child (with Big Ten):   You heard me! The Big Ten!

Children: What's the Big Ten?

Child (with Big Ten):   The Ten Commandments!

Children: The Ten Commandments?

Child (with Big Ten):   That's right, the Ten Commandments!

Child (with First Com.):   I'm number 1!

Children: What's number 1?

Child (with First Com.):   Worship only God!

Child (with Big Ten):   That's the first Commandment.

Children: Got it! Worship only God!

Child (with Second Com.):   I'm number 2!

Children: What's number 2?

Child (with Second Com.): Do not worship things.

Child (with Big Ten): That's the second Commandment.

Children: Got it! Do not worship things!

Continue with this pattern until all of Ten Commandments have been introduced. Finish the litany by having the kids holding the Commandments line up facing the group.

Child (with Big Ten): Let's say them all again.

Child 1: Worship only God!

Children: Worship only God!

Child 2: Do not worship things!

Children: Do not worship things!

Continue until all Ten Commandments have been said.

Child (with Big 10): These are God's rules for us!

Children: These are God's rules for us!

Child (with Big 10): Let's hear it for the Big Ten!

Children: YEAH! BIG TEN!

  (*Children jump up and cheer.*)

> ⁂ **Idea** ⁂
> ....
> Play "Let's Hear It Again for the Big 10".

GAME: LET'S HEAR IT AGAIN, FOR THE BIG 10

 MATERIALS: The Ten Commandment cards from "The Big Ten," page 43.

PREPARATION
Hide the cards.

DIRECTIONS
1. Choose ten children to be the "card scouts." They will search for the "Big Ten."

2. Each child is to find one card.

3. After the cards are found, have the scouts stand in any order.

4. See if the "scouts" can put themselves into the correct order.

5. Let the scouts lead the litany, "The Big Ten."

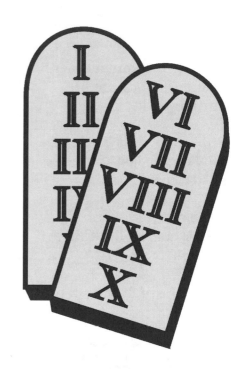

REJOICE AND BE GLAD

 Scripture: Matthew 5:1-12

Read this scripture to the children.

Leader: Blessed are the poor in spirit, for theirs is the kingdom of heaven.

Children: Rejoice and be glad!

Leader: Blessed are those who mourn, for they will be comforted.

Children: Rejoice and be glad.

Leader: Blessed are the meek, for they will inherit the earth.

Children: Rejoice and be glad!

Leader: Blessed are those who hunger and thirst for righteousness, for they will be filled.

Children: Rejoice and be glad!

Leader: Blessed are the merciful, for they will receive mercy.

Children: Rejoice and be glad!

Leader: Blessed are the pure in heart, for they will see God.

Children: Rejoice and be glad!

Leader: Blessed are the peacemakers, for they will be called children of God.

Children: Rejoice and be glad!

Leader: Blessed are those who are persecuted for righteousness' sake, for theirs is the kingdom of heaven.

Children: Rejoice and be glad!

Leader: Blessed are you when people revile you and persecute you and utter all kinds of evil against you falsely on my account.

Children: Rejoice and be glad!

Leader: Your reward is great in heaven.

Children: Rejoice and be glad!

☀ Ideas ☀

1. Give the children rhythm instruments. Let them play the instruments during the response.

2. Clap and cheer each time "Rejoice and be glad!" is spoken.

3. Use this format for other passages of scripture you want to highlight with the children.

COME FOLLOW ME

 Scripture: Matthew 4:19

DIRECTIONS

1. Ask a volunteer to portray Jesus.

2. Jesus will go up to each child, calling them by name, and asking them to follow him.

3. Have children engaged in activities throughout the room. When they are called by Jesus, they will stop the activity and leave it to follow Jesus.

4. Continue with the litany until all children are "followers."

Jesus: (Child's name), I need a helper. Come, follow me.

Melissa: Okay, Jesus. I will follow you.

Jesus: (Child's name), I need a helper. Come follow me.

Benjamin: Okay, Jesus. I will follow you.

To end the litany:

Jesus: Let the children come to me. I will make you fishers of people.

Children: Okay, Jesus. I will follow you.

✳ Ideas ✳

1. As Jesus and the children are "gathering" disciples, have Jesus play "Follow the Leader." Jesus will do something and the children must mimic it.

2. Let the children take turns portraying Jesus.

3. Let the children help Jesus gather followers.

LET'S GO LOOK FOR THAT SHEEP!

 Scripture: Luke 15:3-6

Tell this as a story to the children:

There was a shepherd who had 100 sheep. One day, one of the sheep wandered away and got lost. The shepherd went to look for his lost sheep. He looked and looked and looked. Finally, he found the lost sheep. The sheep was really frightened. The shepherd was so happy to find his sheep, that he picked it up and gently placed it on his shoulders. When he got home, he put the sheep back in the pasture. He told all of his friends that he had found his lost sheep.

Leader: A sheep is lost.

Children: A sheep is lost.

Leader: Gotta go find that sheep.

Children: Gotta go find that sheep.

Leader: Let's go look for that sheep.

Children: Let's go look for that sheep.

(Use hands to make walking steps on your thighs.)

Leader: Look! Look! There's a tree! *(Look, point)*

Children: Look! Look! There's a tree! *(Look, point)*

Leader: Let's climb up it.

Children: Let's climb up it.

(Use hands to make climbing motion.)

Leader: Look around! Look around! *(Looking motion)*

Children: Look around! Look around! (*Looking motion*)

Leader: I sure don't see that sheep!

Children: I sure don't see that sheep!

Leader: Let's climb down.

Children: Let's climb down.

(*Use hands to make climbing motion.*)

(*Use hands to make walking steps on your thighs.*)

Leader: Look! Look! There's a lake! (*Look, point*)

Children: Look! Look! There's a lake! (*Look, point*)

Leader: Let's swim across!

Children: Let's swim across!

(*Use hands to make swimming motion.*)

Leader: Let's get out of the water. (*Get out.*)

Children: Let's get out of the water. (*Get out.*)

(*Use hands to make walking steps on your thighs.*)

Leader: Look! Look! There are some bulrushes! (*Look, point*)

Children: Look! Look! There are some bulrushes! (*Look, point*)

Leader: Let's walk through them.

Children: Let's walk through them.

(*Use hands to make a forward swishing motion.*)

Leader: We got through them.

Children: We got through them.

(*Use hands to make walking steps on your thighs.*)

Leader: Look! Look! There's a cliff! (*Point, look*)

Children: Look! Look! There's a cliff! (*Point, look*)

Leader: Let's climb to the top!

Children: Let's climb to the top.

(*Make climbing motions.*)

Leader: We're on top of the cliff. Look around! (*Look*)

Children: We're on top of the cliff. Look around! (*Look*)

Leader: Look! Look! I see a sheep! (*Point, look*)

Children: Look! Look! I see a sheep! (*Point, look*)

Leader: Let's go get him.

Children: Let's go get him.

(*Walk on thighs. Pick up sheep. Put sheep on shoulders. Walk on thighs.*)

Leader: Let's take him home.

Children: Let's take him home.

(*Reverse the direction of the sheep hunt. Climb down the cliff, wade through the bulrushes, swim across the lake, climb up the tree, and climb down the tree. Say all of the lines, do all of the motions.*)

Leader: Let's put the sheep into his pasture.

Children: Let's put the sheep into his pasture.

Leader: He's happy to be home.

Children: He's happy to be home.

> ☀ **Idea** ☀
>
> Use with "Help the Shepherd Find His Lost Sheep" maze on page 48.

PUZZLE
MAZE: HELP THE SHEPHERD FIND HIS LOST SHEEP

IT'S A MIRACLE

 Scripture: John 3:2

DIRECTIONS

1. Have the children position themselves around the room.

2. The first time they say the response, it should be in a whisper. Each time they say the response, it should get louder and louder until the final response is shouted!

Leader:	Jesus fed five thousand people!
Children:	Oh, wow! It's a miracle!
Leader:	Jesus made a blind man see!
Children:	Oh, wow! It's a miracle!
Leader:	Jesus calmed a raging storm.
Children:	Oh, wow! It's a miracle!
Leader:	Jesus walked on water!
Children:	Oh, wow! It's a miracle!
Leader:	Jesus raised Lazarus from the dead!
Children:	Oh, wow! It's a miracle!
Leader:	Jesus rose from the dead!
Children:	Oh, wow! It's a miracle!
Leader:	Jesus lives forever!
Children:	Oh, wow! It's a miracle!
All:	JESUS LIVES FOREVER! OH, WOW! IT'S A MIRACLE!

☀ Ideas ☀

1. Add other miracles to the litany.

2. On Easter Sunday, let the children share this litany during the adult worship service. Have the children scatter themselves along the walls, around the altar, and other places in the sanctuary. As each miracle is spoken, let one or several children jump out and say the response.

3. Use with the "Worship Talk About Easter" on pages 130-31.

O GIVE THANKS

 Scripture: Psalm 107:1

MATERIALS: Very large cornucopia (can be made or purchased from craft stores); objects we are thankful for which will fit into the cornucopia (fruits, toys, clothes, books, and so forth—one object per child); blindfold (optional for younger children)

PREPARATION
Gather the objects and put them into the cornucopia.

DIRECTIONS

1. Sit in a circle with the children, with the cornucopia in front of you.

2. One at a time, blindfold each child and invite him or her to pull an object from the cornucopia.

3. Give thanks for that object.

4. Do the litany as a rap. Alternate clapping and thigh slapping as you recite the litany.

Leader:	O give thanks to the Lord.
Child 1:	Thank you, God, for giving us books.
Children:	Thanks be to God! Yeah, God! *(Raise arms overhead.)*
Leader:	O give thanks to the Lord.
Child 2:	Thank you, God, for giving us apples.

☀ Ideas ☀

1. Share the litany during a Thanksgiving worship service. Let the congregation take part in the response: "Thanks be to God! Yeah, God!!" Be sure to take your "Cornucopia of Blessings!"

2. Use with the "Thanksgiving Worship Talk" on page 134, call to worship on pages 25-26, prayers on page 74, and benedictions on page 100.

Children: Thanks be to God. Yeah, God!!

(Raise arms overhead.)

Continue with this format until each child has had a turn. End the litany with:

Leader: O give thanks to the Lord, for he is good. His steadfast love endures forever.

Children: O give thanks to the Lord, for he is good. His steadfast love endures forever! Yeah, God!!

(Jump up, clap, and cheer.)

※ Hint ※

For ideas on how to rap, ask a child or teenager to demonstrate.

GLORY TO GOD

 Scripture: Luke 2:1-20

Tell the story of Jesus' birth.

MATERIALS: One picture of each of the things mentioned in the litany, one piece of construction paper per picture, scissors, glue, Contact paper

PREPARATION
1. Glue each picture to a piece of construction paper.

2. Cover with Contact paper.

DIRECTIONS
1. Sit in a circle with the children.

2. Give each child a picture. Keep the pictures in the order of the litany.

3. Have each child hold up the picture at the appropriate time.

Leader: A baby was born in a stable tonight.

Children: Glory to God in the highest!

Leader: They named the baby Jesus.

Children: Glory to God in the highest!

Leader: A bright star shone in the sky.

Children: Glory to God in the highest!

Leader: The angels sang songs of glory!

Children: Glory to God in the highest!

Leader: The shepherds came to worship the King.

Children: Glory to God in the highest!

Leader: The Wise Men came to bring him gifts.

Children: Glory to God in the highest!

Leader: Jesus was sent to be our Savior.

Children: Glory to God in the highest!

※ Hint ※

1. Coloring books provide good pictures. Purchase two copies. Color the pictures, and cut them out.

2. If you have more children than pictures, make stars for them. Cover the stars with glitter. Attach each star to a dowel rod. Let the children hold up the stars during the response.

PUZZLE:
JESUS LOVES YOU

Color: B: blue
R: red

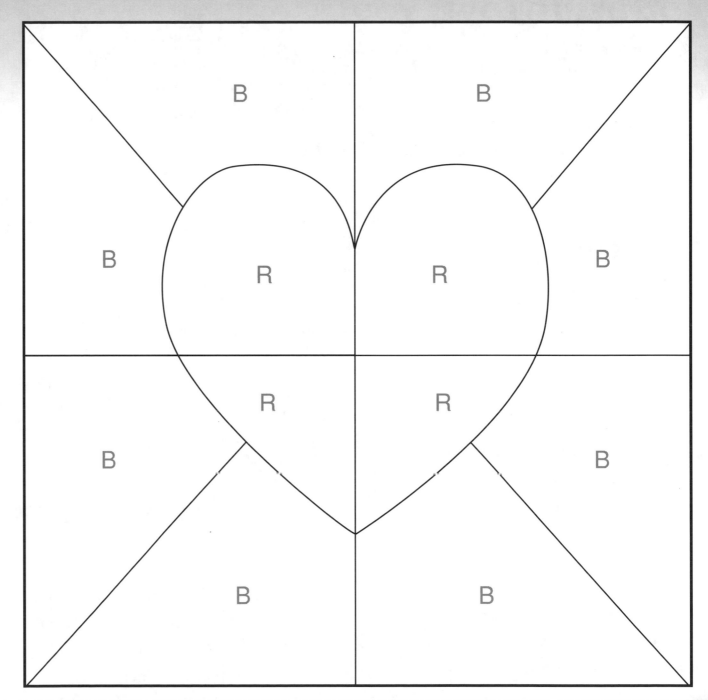

GOD (JESUS) LOVES YOU

 Scripture: John 15:9

God (Jesus) loves you.   *(Point to others.)*

God (Jesus) loves me.   *(Point to self.)*

God (Jesus) loves everyone   *(Point to all.)*

We see.   *(Point to self, point to eyes.)*

Idea

Sing "Jesus Loves Me."

I LOVE JESUS!

 Scripture: Ephesians 5:1

Leader:	I love Jesus!
Children:	I love Jesus!
Leader:	Jesus is God's son.
Children:	Jesus is God's son.
Leader:	He was born in Bethlehem.
Children:	He was born in Bethlehem.
Leader:	Jesus taught us how to live.
Children:	Jesus taught us how to live.
Leader:	Jesus came to help us.
Children:	Jesus came to help us.
Leader:	Jesus died upon the cross.
Children:	Jesus died upon the cross.
Leader:	To save us from our sins.
Children:	To save us from our sins.
Leader:	Jesus loves us all.
Children:	Jesus loves us all.
Leader:	I love Jesus!
Children:	I love Jesus!

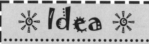
Idea

Clap the rhythm of the words with the children after their response.

GOD IS MY FRIEND

 Scripture: Proverbs 18:24

God is my friend.   *(Point to self.)*

And yours too.   *(Point to others.)*

God is with us,   *(Hold out hands.)*

In all we do.   *(Place hands over heart.)*

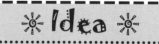
Idea

Make a song using the tune "Frere Jacques," and sing each line twice.

MAZE: LET'S FIND JESUS

Help the kids find Jesus.

JESUS HELPS US

 Scripture: Hebrews 13:6

Jesus helps us in all we do.
Jesus helps me, and Jesus helps you.
Jesus helps us know how to live.
Jesus taught us to forgive.
I love Jesus, I really do.
And I hope you love him too.

☀ Ideas ☀

1. Sing this to "Twinkle, Twinkle Little Star."

2. Think of motions to accompany this affirmation.

3. Use with "Let's Find Jesus" on page 53.

LET'S FOLLOW JESUS

 Scripture: Luke 9:57

DIRECTIONS

Ask a volunteer to portray Jesus. Have Jesus ask the children to do all sorts of things to illustrate that they follow him.

Jesus: If you want to follow me say, "Let's follow Jesus," and clap your hands.

Children: Let's follow Jesus. (*Clap hands.*)

Jesus: If you want to follow me say, "Let's follow Jesus," and stamp your feet.

Children: Let's follow Jesus. (*Stamp feet.*)

To end the affirmation say:

Jesus: If you want to follow me say, "Let's follow Jesus," and sit down here.

Children: Let's follow Jesus. (*Sit down.*)

I BELIEVE

 Scripture: Genesis 1:2—2:3

Tell the story of Creation to the children.

MATERIALS: Pictures of things God created placed in a basket

DIRECTIONS
1. Put the pictures face down in the basket.

2. Sit in a circle with the children.

3. Keep the space to your right vacant.

4. Let each child come, individually, and sit on your right. That child takes the top picture from the basket and holds it up for everyone to see.

Leader:	I believe God created butterflies.
Children:	I believe God created butterflies.
All:	Yeah, God!
Leader:	I believe God created clouds.
Children:	I believe God created clouds.
All:	Yeah, God!

To end the affirmation.

Leader:	I believe God created the whole world.
Children:	I believe God created the whole world.
All:	Yeah, God!

I BELIEVE IN GOD

 Scripture: John 9:38

I believe, I believe, I believe in God!
I believe, I believe, I believe God loves you and me!
I believe, I believe, I believe God cares for everyone!
I believe, I believe, I believe that God is good!

Say this as a rap. Give two quick claps at the end of each line.

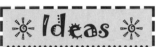

☀ Ideas ☀

1. Begin each line very softly gradually becoming louder by the end of the sentence.

2. Begin the affirmation in a very soft whisper, letting the whisper become louder until you are speaking in a soft voice which gradually becomes louder until you are shouting when you reach, "I believe that God is good!"

PUZZLE: WHO DO YOU BELIEVE?

 Follow each set of dots to find the answer.

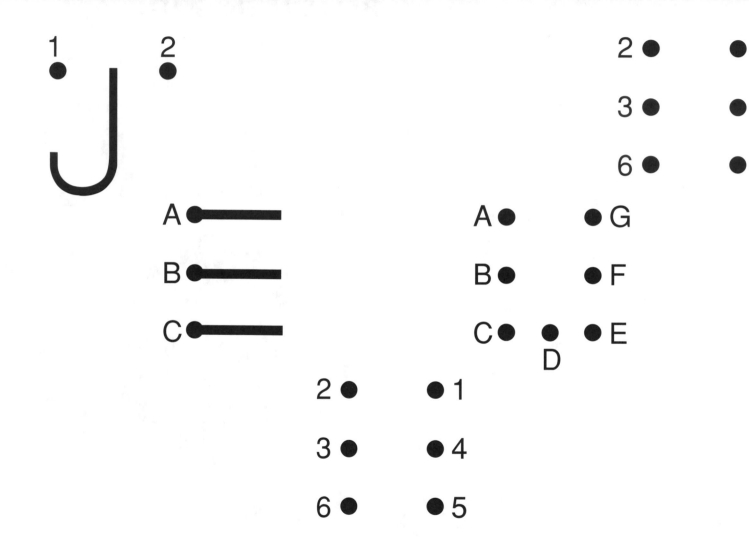

GOD IS MY LIGHT, CHRIST IS MY SAVIOR

 Scripture: John 12:46

MATERIALS: One battery-operated candle.

DIRECTIONS

1. Stand in a circle with the children.

2. Turn off the lights in the room and turn on the candle.

3. Before beginning, talk about how God "lights the way" for us to follow Christ our Savior.

Leader:	God created the world. God created night and day; darkness and light.
Children:	God is my light.
Leader:	God gave us rules to follow, so we would know how to live.
Children:	God is my light.
Leader:	God sent Jesus to teach us how to live and be our Savior.
Children:	Christ is my Savior.
Leader:	Christ died on the cross to save us from our sins.
Children:	Christ is my Savior.

 Ideas

1. For older children (8-10 year olds), use a real candle. Explain the importance of safety while using lighted candles. Use Christmas candlelight service candles, and illustrate the proper way to hold a lighted candle.
2. Give each child a candle and do the above ceremony with one change. The leader stands in the center of the circle and moves to each child saying:
3. Use your candle to light the child's candle. Repeat the following lines with each child in the circle.
4. When all the candles are lit, raise the candles and say, **"God is my light, Christ is my Savior."**
5. Pause and extinguish the candles.

Hold the candle up high and say: "God is my light, Christ is my Savior."(*Pass the candle to the right.*) The child next to the leader will hold the candle up high and say, "God is my light, Christ is my Savior." Keep passing the candle to the right, making the affirmation while holding the candle high overhead. When the candle returns to the leader, everyone will respond with the affirmation together.

All:	God is my light, Christ is my Savior.
Leader:	(Name), you are created in God's image, which is good.
Child:	God is my light, Christ is my Savior.

 VARIATION:

Instead of real candles, let each child hold the battery-operated candle while being affirmed.

CREATOR, CHRIST, AND LIVING SPIRIT

 Scripture: John 14:1

I believe in God, the Creator who created a world of beauty for us to love, care for, and enjoy.

I believe that God sent Jesus Christ to earth to teach us how to live the way God wants us to live.

I believe that Christ lived among people and taught them how to live according to God's rules.

I believe that Christ died on the cross at Calvary to save us from our sins.

I believe that Jesus Christ is my savior.

I believe that the Living Spirit lives among us, caring for us and guiding us, never leaving us alone.

I believe that I am God's child, created in God's image which is good.

I believe in the Creator, Christ, and Living Spirit.

※ Ideas ※

1. Use wide-tipped, colorful markers to write each sentence of the affirmation on a piece of white construction paper. Number them on the back to easily keep them in the proper sequence. Cover the pages with clear Contact paper.

2. Have the children sit in a circle. Give a piece of paper to each child, making sure to keep affirmation in the proper order. Have the children hold the papers up so everyone can see them.

3. Have the entire group read the affirmation together.

4. Use with "A Shamrock Trinity" on page 59.

PUZZLE: A SHAMROCK TRINITY

St. Patrick used the shamrock to teach people about the Trinity. Unscramble each word and print the circled letters here _____.
Unscramble the letters, and print the word in the spaces inside the shamrock. Color the shamrock green.

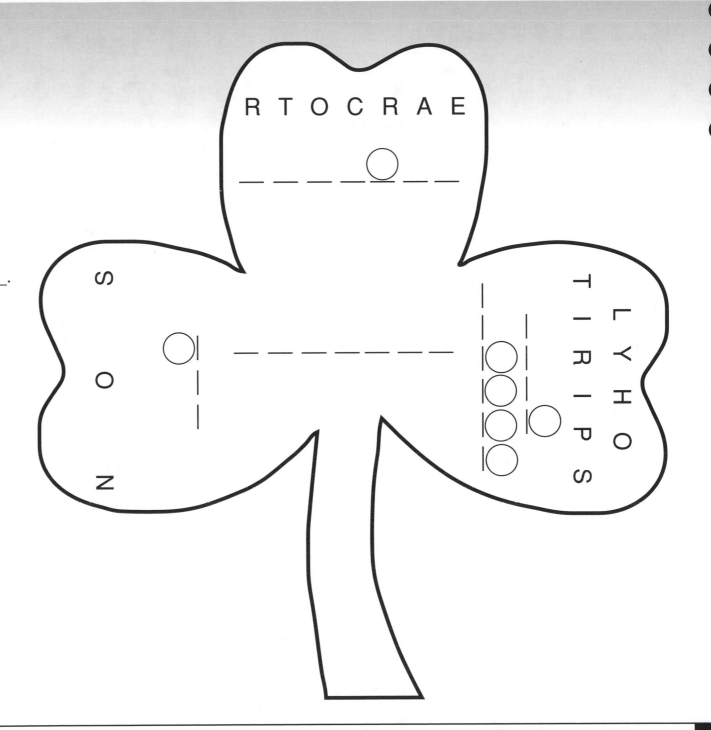

WHAT DO I BELIEVE?

Scripture: Romans 10:9

MATERIALS: 1 scripture pencil (or other object) per child

DIRECTIONS

1. Stand in a circle with the children, and let each child have a turn to share their beliefs.

2. Give the children a pencil when they state their beliefs.

Leader: (Child), what do you believe about God?

Child 1: (example: I believe God created animals.)

Leader: (Child), what do you believe about Jesus?

Child 2: (example: I believe Jesus was God's son.)

☀ Ideas ☀

1. Use this as a model to create an affirmation written by the children. Give each child paper and crayons, and ask them to draw pictures of what they believe about God and Jesus. They can show these during the affirmation.

2. Make a book of the children's affirmations. Ask one person to create an attractive cover. Staple the pages together. Put the book into the children's resource center or church library.

AFFIRMATION CEREMONIES

These ceremonies allow you to affirm the children in your ministry.

I AM A CHILD OF CHRIST

Scripture: John 12:36

MATERIALS: Cross pattern on page 95, paper punch, yarn, crayons, glitter, tissue paper, glue, cassette tape player and tape of soothing instrumental music

PREPARATION

1. Punch a hole in the top of each cross.

2. String each cross with yarn long enough to slip over a child's head.

DIRECTIONS

1. Let the children decorate their crosses using the crayons, glitter, and tissue paper.

2. Teach the responsive line to the children prior to the ceremony.

3. Dim the lights and play the music.

4. Have the children stand in a circle holding their crosses.

Leader: You are all children of Christ.

Children: We are all children of Christ.

Leader: We come to affirm these children, Lord.

Children: We are all children of Christ.

Leader: God, you created each of these children.

Each child is special.

Children: We are all children of Christ.

Move clockwise around the circle. Have each child hold his or her cross high and say:

Child: "My name is
(child's name).
I am a child of Christ
who died on the
cross for me."

Hint

For preschool children follow this pattern:

Child: My name is
(child's name).
Leader: (Child's name), you
are a child of Christ.

As the children finish their individual affirmation, they may slip the cross over their head, so it hangs around their neck. Conclude by saying:

Leader: Thank you God for creating these children.

All: We are all children of Christ. Amen.

I AM A CHILD OF GOD

 Scripture: Galatians 3:26

Follow the instructions on page 60 for making the crosses. Have the children stand in a circle, darken the room and play soft instrumental music.

Leader: These are the children of the Lord.

Children: I am a child of God.

Leader: Lord, you created each child in your image.

Children: I am a child of God.

Leader: Each child here is special and unique.

Children: I am a child of God.

Stand behind one of the children and place your hands on the child's shoulders. Say something special about that child. (Example: Kerry is kind to new children who visit with us.) When you finish, the child will say: "I am a child of God."

The rest of the children will respond with, "Thank you God, for (child's name)."

Slip the cross over the child's head, so it hangs around the child's neck.

When you have affirmed each child conclude with:

Leader: Thank you God for each of these children.

Children: I am a child of God. Amen.

Chapter 3: Prayers

Prayers are what we say to God. When we pray we ask God to help us and give us what we need. We can use prayers to thank God for what he has given to us or done for us.

Using "repeat after me" prayers can be tricky, since children will often continue to "repeat" even after the prayer has concluded. One way to avoid this problem is to have a "responsive sentence" that is spoken at certain points throughout a prayer and that is used only with the prayer.

Active and quiet time prayers are included here. Experiment with brief times of silent prayer, telling the children that silent prayers allow us to talk to God all by ourselves and at any time we choose. A silent prayer can be said just before a test, just before a game, when we are waiting in line, and so on. God is ready to listen to us whenever we want to talk.

Prayer responses are musical continuations of a spoken prayer. Sometimes a time of prayer is begun with a song that helps prepare us to speak our prayers. This is known as a *call to prayer*. The prayer responses included here can also be used in that way. The word *AMEN* means "so be it." That means we want God to answer our prayers in the way that God thinks is best for us. We have to trust that God knows what is best for us.

Praying with children is rewarding because they are so honest and open when they talk to God. Cherish their love of the Lord as you share times of prayer with them.

☀ Responsive Sentences ☀
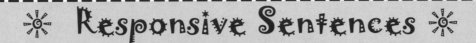

Hear us, my Lord.	(Genesis 23:6)
God is our strength.	(Psalm 46:1)
It is good to give thanks to the Lord.	(Psalm 92:1)
Make a joyful noise to the Lord.	(Psalm 100:1)
Worship the Lord with gladness.	(Psalm 100:2)
Hear our prayer, O Lord.	(Psalm 102:1)
Help me, O Lord my God.	(Psalm 109:26)
The Lord is near to all who call.	(Psalm 145:8, adapted)
The Lord is good to all.	(Psalm 145:9)
Praise the Lord!	(Psalm 150:1)
Give thanks to the Lord!	(Isaiah 12:4)
God is with us.	(Matthew 1:23)
Glory to God in the highest.	(Luke 2:14)
Peace be with you.	(Luke 24:36)
The God of peace be with you.	(Romans 15:33)

HEAR OUR PRAYER

 Scripture: Psalm 102:1

Invite the children to sit on a cozy rug with you. Begin by asking the children to share prayer concerns (Does anyone have a test coming up this week? Is anyone in your family sick? Are you worried about anything?).

Incorporate the requests into a prayer. After each request is shared, the children may respond with, "Hear our prayer, O Lord."

 Example:

Leader: Creator God, thank you for this time together. Thank you for this new day. Thank you for taking good care of us.

Children: Hear our prayer, OLord.

Leader: Please be with (child's name)'s daddy while he is away on business. Take good care of him. Bring him home soon.

Children: Hear our prayer, OLord.

Leader: God, help (child's name)'s uncle get better soon.

Children: Hear our prayer, O Lord.

All: AMEN!

 Example:

Leader: Creator God, thank you for bringing us all together this week. Thank you for this new day. Help us to remember that you are always with us wherever we go.

Children: Hear our prayer, O Lord.

Leader: God, please be with (child's name) as she takes her math test. Help all of our children to study hard and to do the best they can in school. You know, God, some-times it is tempting to cheat on a test. Help us to avoid the temptation of cheating and to be honest in our work.

Children: Hear our prayer, O Lord.

Leader: God, stay close to (child's name) and her family this week. (Child's name)'s grandmother is having surgery. That's scary, God. Please let (child's name), her family, and her grandmother feel your presence.

Children: Hear our prayer, O Lord.

Leader: Please, God, help (child's name) face the bully at school with courage. Please help him not to be so afraid and help (child's name) to feel your love and strength.

Children: Hear our prayer, O Lord.

Leader: God, bless each of these children. They are all special and precious. Help them live according to your rules.

Children: Hear our prayer, O Lord.

Leader: Dear Lord, help me to teach these children about you and your love for us.

Children: Hear our prayer, O Lord.

Leader: God, you have heard our prayers. You know what we need. We thank you for loving us and caring for us. In the name of the Creator, the Christ, and the living Spirit, we pray.

All: AMEN.

☀ Ideas ☀

1. Combine this with the "Bubble Prayers" on page 82 or "Play Ball" on page 84.
2. Before you begin, sing "We Come to Pray to You Today" on page 73.
3. At the conclusion of the prayer sing, "Hear Us as We Pray" on page 72.
4. Use with "Let's Pray" on pages 67.

PUZZLE:
WHAT DOES GOD WANT US TO DO?

Color   P: Purple
            O: Orange

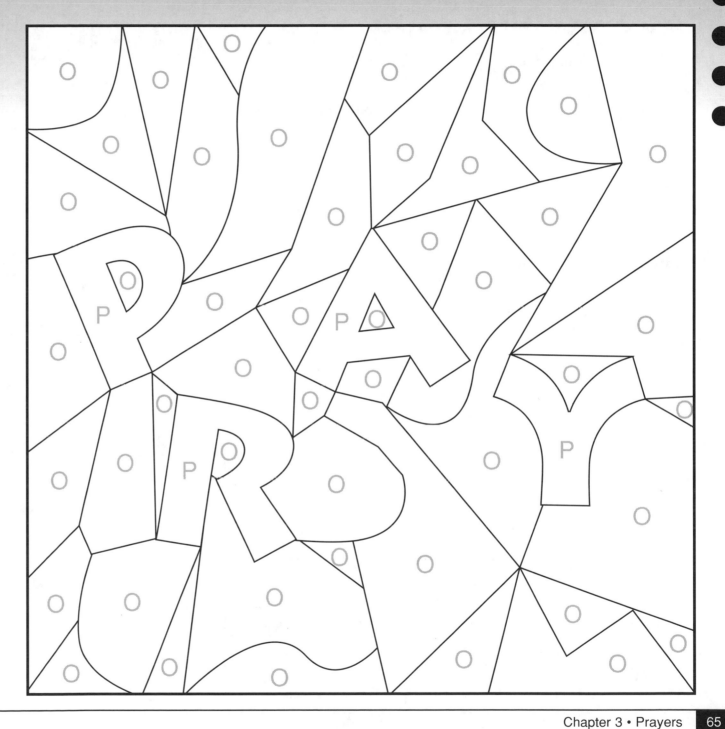

GOOD MORNING, GOD!

 Scripture: Titus 3:15

This prayer is a nice way to open a group time with children.

Leader: Good morning (afternoon, evening), God!

Children: Bless us, O Lord!

Leader: Thank you for bringing these children to church (Sunday school, school, choir, other).

Children: Bless us, O Lord!

Leader: Let us enjoy our time together.

Children: Bless us, O Lord!

Leader: Help us to learn more about you.

Children: Bless us, O Lord!

Leader: Help us to remember that you love us.

Children: Bless us, O Lord!

Leader: Help us to be kind to other people.

Children: Bless us, O Lord!

All: BLESS US, O LORD! AMEN!

❉ Ideas ❉

1. After this prayer sing one of the responses on pages 72-73.

2. Combine this with "When We Pray" on page 81 or "Bounce It!" on pages 84.

❉ Hint ❉

Create your own special prayers for your group using this pattern. Keep the children's response the same throughout the prayer.

PUZZLE: LET'S PRAY

There are many things we can pray for. God listens to all of our prayer requests. God gives us just what we need. Read each sentence. Unscramble the word to fit the blank space.

1. We can ask God to (ELHP) ___ ___ ___ ◯ us to do our best in school.

2. When we do something wrong, we can ask God to (GIVEFOR) ___ ___ ◯ ___ ___ ___ ___ us.

3. When we are (FRAAID) ___ ___ ___ ◯ ___ ___ we can ask God to help us.

4. God loves (OUY) ◯ ___ ___.

5. We can ask God to stay (HITW) ◯ ___ ___ ___ us wherever we go.

6. Remember, that Jesus came to be our (VIORSA) ___ ___ ___ ◯ ___ ___.

7. We should ask God to help our (CHTEARES) ◯ ___ ___ ___ ___ ___ ___ ___ at (CHSOOL) ___ ___ ◯ ___ ___ ___.

8. We can ask God to give us (DOFO) ___ ◯ ___ ___.

9. Remember, God will stay with you during a scary (STORMTHUNDER) ___ ___ ◯ ___ ___ ___ ___ ___ ◯ ___ ___ ___.

10. We can ask God to give us the (THCLOES) ◯ ___ ___ ___ ___ ___ we need to wear.

11. We can ask God to give us a (MOHE) ___ ___ ___ ◯.

12. Remember, God (WAYSAL) ___ ___ ___ ◯ ___ ___ loves us.

13. God likes to hear us (GNIS) ◯ ___ ___ ___ prayers.

14. We should ask God to help us do what is (GHRIT) ___ ◯ ___ ___ ___.

15. God (DEENS) ◯ ___ ___ ___ ___ all of us.

16. Remember that (DOG) ◯ ___ ___ is your friend.

Write the circled letters in the spaces below.

___ ___ ___ ___ ___ ___   ___ ___ ___ ___ ___ ___ ___

(1 SALONTHESIANS) ___ ___ ___ ___ ___ ___ ___ ___ ___ ___ ___ ___ ___ ___   5:17   What does this verse mean?

WELCOME

 Scripture: Matthew 25:35

Use this prayer to welcome new or visiting children.

Leader: Hi, God! Thanks for bringing us together today. Thank you for bringing (child's name) to us today, God.

Children: Welcome, (child's name)!

Leader: Let (child's name) feel the love we have for one another.

Children: Welcome, (child's name)!

Leader: Let us show your love to (child's name).

Children: Welcome, (child's name)!

Leader: Bring (child's name) back to us again, God.

Children: Welcome, (child's name)!

All: Welcome, (child's name). We are glad you are here. Praise the Lord. AMEN!

✳ Ideas ✳

Sing "Welcome" on page 17.

A NEW SCHOOL YEAR

 Scripture: Luke 2:40

Talk to the children about the upcoming school year. Encourage them to share their feelings. Incorporate their thoughts into your prayer.

Leader: Dear Lord, it's the beginning of a new school year.

Children: Help us to learn, O Lord.

Leader: God, help us to do our best to learn all of the new things that will be taught to us.

Children: Help us to learn, O Lord.

Leader: Help us to be honest in our work, God. Keep us from the temptation of cheating.

Children: Help us to learn, O Lord.

Leader: Give us the strength to study, Lord. Help us remember that school is important.

Children: Help us to learn, O Lord.

Leader: Let us be polite to our teachers. Help us to follow the rules.

Children: Help us to learn, O Lord.

Leader: God, help us to be kind to all of the children at school. Let us make friends with kids who don't seem to have many friends.

✳ Ideas ✳

1. See page 144 for "Happy New School Year."

2. Sing one of the prayer responses in this section.

Children: Help us to learn, O Lord.

Leader: God, please bless each of these children. Please be with each of them as they begin school this week. Please take away any fears and doubts they have. Let them know you are sitting right beside them. Let them remember that you love them. Help them to know what you want them to do the best they can.

Children: Help us to learn, O Lord.

Leader: God, we know that you love us and care for us. Help the children know that you love them. In your holy name, we pray.

All: AMEN!

GET WELL SOON

 Scripture: Psalm 102:1

Leader: Dear Lord, (child's name) is not with us today. (Child's name) is at home (in the hospital) with (name illness/injury).

Children: Hear our prayer, O Lord.

Leader: Please take care of (child's name), God.

Children: Hear our prayer, O Lord.

Leader: Please help the doctors who are taking care of him/her. Help them as they care for (child's name).

Children: Hear our prayer, O Lord.

Leader: Please be with (child's name)'s family (parents, brothers, sisters), God. Let them feel your love. Let them know you are there to help them.

Children: Hear our prayer, O Lord.

Leader: Help (child's name), God. Let him/her feel your strength. Let him/her get well soon, so he/she can come back and be with us.

Children: Hear our prayer, O Lord.

All: AMEN.

> ☀ **Idea** ☀
> ....
> Sing "Please Be with Us" on page 72.

SOMEONE SPECIAL

 Scripture: Psalm 23

Read the entire Psalm to the children.

Leader: Dear God, we are very sad today.

Children: Be with us as we pray.

Leader: (Child's name) died. That makes us feel sad.

Children: Be with us as we pray.

Leader: Help us to remember all of the good things about (child's name).

Children: Be with us as we pray.

Leader: Let us remember how (child's name) (list things this person did, things that made this person special).

Children: Be with us as we pray.

Leader: God, we know that you understand our sadness. Stay close to us and help us.

Children: Be with us as we pray.

Leader: Help us remember that nothing bad can ever happen to (child's name). He/she is in your care now. We know that you will take good care of him/her.

Children: Be with us as we pray.

All: Be with us as we pray, God. AMEN.

☀ Ideas ☀

1. Have the children draw pictures and write something special about the person who has died. Have one of the children design an attractive cover. Staple the pages together to make a book. Give this book to the child's family.

2. See pages 143-44 for "Death Brings New Life."

PUZZLE: WHAT SHOULD WE DO?

Unscramble the words and print them in the spaces to the right. Print the circled letter from each word in the space on the left.

___ FULJOY ( )___ ___ ___ ___ ___

___ CUHRCH ___ ___ ( )___ ___ ___

___ SEHTOLC ___ ___ ___ ___ ___ ( )

___ CHATEERS ( )___ ___ ___ ___ ___ ___

___ MAFILY ___ ( )___ ___ ___ ___

___ COOLSH ( )___ ___ ___ ___

___ THERO SKID ___ ___ ___ ___ ___ ( )___ ___ ___

___ NESSGIVEFOR ___ ___ ___ ( )___ ___ ___ ___ ___ ___ ___

___ TORASP ___ ___ ___ ( )___

___ FODO ___ ___ ( )___

HEAR US AS WE PRAY

 Scripture: Psalm 102:1

 (Sung to "Twinkle, Twinkle")

Hear us as we pray, O Lord.

Hear the prayers we pray to you.

Be with us as we pray.

Help us each and every day.

Hear us as we pray, O Lord.

Hear the prayers we pray to you.

LISTEN GOD

 Scripture: Psalm 5:2

 (Sung to "Frere Jacques")

Listen God.

Listen God.

As we pray.

As we pray.

We pray for peace and love.

We pray for peace and love.

Amen.

Amen.

PLEASE BE WITH US

 Scripture: Matthew 1:23

 (Sung to "Mary Had a Little Lamb")

Please be with us as we pray, as we pray, as we pray.

Please be with us as we pray,

Each and every day.

LORD, HEAR US

 Scripture: Psalm 55:1

 (Sung to "Skip to My Lou")

Lord, Lord, Lord hear us.

Lord, Lord, Lord hear us.

Lord, Lord, Lord hear us.

Hear us as we pray!

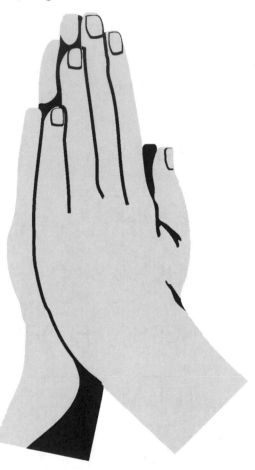

☀ Idea ☀

Encourage the children to think of things we might add. Change lines 5 and 6 to accommodate their ideas.

WE COME TO PRAY TO YOU TODAY

 Scripture: Psalm 88:2

 (Sung to "Mulberry Bush")

We come to pray to you today,
to you today, to you today.
We come to pray to you today.
Hear us, loving Jesus.

✳ Idea ✳

Sing this before "Hear Our Prayer" on page 64.

 **SOMETHING SPECIAL**

Sing one of these prayer responses after the morning prayer. Or during Sunday morning worship have the children's choir sing one of these prayer responses.

"Oh, Bless the Lord My Soul,"

by Ken Medema

"Jesus, Name Above All Names,"

by Naida Hearn

"Father Lift Me Up,"

by Honeytree

(From *Sing 'n' Celebrate for Kids*, vol. 2, by Milton Okan)

WE GIVE YOU OUR GIFTS

 Scripture: James 1:17

God, these are the gifts we give to you today. Please use these gifts to help those who need your help. AMEN!

OUR GIFT TO YOU

 Scripture: Acts 20:32

God, please acccpt the offerings we bring. We hope that our gifts will help other people. They are our gift to you. AMEN!

WE COME TO GIVE OUR GIFTS

 Scripture: Acts 20:32

 (Sung to "Mulberry Bush")

We come to give our gifts today, our gifts today,
our gifts today.
We come to give our gifts today.
We give our gifts to God.

THANKS, THANKS, THANKS TO GOD

 Scripture: James 1:17

 (Sung to "Row, Row, Row Your Boat")

Thanks, thanks, thanks to God.
For our many blessings.
We come to you with these gifts
To show our love for God.

FOR OUR BLESSINGS, WE GIVE THANKS

 Scripture: Psalm 106:1

 (Sung to "Old MacDonald")

For our blessings we give thanks,
Thank you, thank you, God.
For a thank you here. (clap left)
And a thank you there. (clap right)
Here a thanks. (clap up high)
There a thanks. (clap down low)
Everywhere a thank you.
For our blessings we give thanks.
Thank you, thank you, God.

PRAISE, PRAISE, PRAISE THE LORD

 Scripture: Psalm 111:1

(Sung to "Skip, Skip, Skip to My Lou")

Praise, praise, praise the Lord!
Praise, praise, praise the Lord!
Praise, praise, praise the Lord!
I thank God with my heart!

EASTER ALLELUIA

 Scripture: Matthew 28:6

Leader: Thank you, God, for such good news!
Children: Alleluia!
Leader: Christ has risen!
Children: Alleluia!
Leader: Christ will live with us forever!
Children: Alleluia!
All: CHRIST HAS RISEN! ALLELUIA!!

CHRIST HAS RISEN

 Scripture: Matthew 28:6

Glory to God for sending us his Son. Thanks be to Christ for loving us, for teaching us, and for dying for us. The spirit of the Lord will live in us, forever! Alleluia! Christ has risen!

See pages 130-31 for "Jesus Lives," pages 23-24 for calls to worship, and page 100 for Easter benedictions.

LET US SING ALLELUIA!

 Scripture: Matthew 28:6

 (Sung to "London Bridge")

Let us sing, Alleluia, Alleluia, Alleluia!
Let us sing, Alleluia!
Christ the Lord has risen!

WE COME TO PRAISE THE LORD

 Scripture: Matthew 28:6

 (Sung to "Farmer in the Dell")

We come to praise the Lord!
We come to praise the Lord!
Alleluia! Christ is risen!
We come to praise the Lord!

LET'S HEAR IT FOR OUR MOMS (DADS)

 Scripture: Exodus 20:12

Leader: Let's hear it for our moms (dads).

Children: Yeah, Mom (Dad)!

Leader: They make sure we have food to eat!

Children: Yeah, Mom (Dad)!

Leader: They make sure we have clothes to wear!

Children: Yeah, Mom (Dad)!

Leader: They care for us when we are sick!

Children: Yeah, Mom (Dad)!

Leader: They cheer us on at sports events!

Children: Yeah, Mom (Dad)!

Leader: They tuck us in and listen to prayers!

Children: Yeah, Mom (Dad)!

Add other lines the children suggest.

Leader: Thank you, God, for giving us Moms (Dads)!

Children: Thank you, God, for giving us Moms (Dads)!

All: Yeah, Mom (Dad)!

NOTE:
Be sensitive to the wide variety of family situations (single parent, grandparents, blended families, and others). Adapt this prayer to reflect your children's families.

STAND, CLAP, AND SAY THANK YOU

 Scripture: Exodus 20:12

 (Sung to "Pop Goes the Weasel")

We come to worship God today.

We come to praise our mothers/fathers

For all that they have done for us!

Stand, clap, and say, "Thank you!"

(Children stand and clap)

THANK YOU, GOD

 Scripture: Exodus 20:12

 (Sung to "Frere Jacques")

Thank you, God.	Thank you, God.
Thank you, God.	Thank you, God.
For our moms (dads).	For our moms (dads).
For our moms (dads).	For our moms (dads).
They are very special.	We love you very much.
They are very special.	We love you very much.
Thank you, God.	Thank you, God.
Thank you, God.	Thank you, God.

LET'S GIVE THANKS

 Scripture: 2 Corinthians 9:15

MATERIALS: One beanbag per group.

DIRECTIONS

1. Divide the children into several groups. Have the leader stand in the center.

2. Leader will toss the beanbag to one child who will say something he or she is thankful for. The child tosses the bag back to the leader. Continue until all children have had a turn.

Leader: Let's give thanks.

Children: Let's give thanks.

Leader: (Child's name), what are you thankful for?

Child 1: Food and gymnastics!

Children: Thank you, God, for food and gymnastics!

Leader: Let's give thanks.

Children: Let's give thanks.

Leader: (Child's name), what are you thankful for?

Child 2: Fishing!

Children: Thank you, God, for fishing!

End with:

Leader: Let's give thanks.

Children: Let's give thanks.

All: Thank you, God, for all our blessings!

✶ Hint ✶

1. Help younger children think of things to be thankful for.

2. Adjust the distance you stand when tossing the beanbag. Stand closer to younger children and further from older children.

THANKS BE TO GOD

 Scripture: 2 Corinthians 9:15

MATERIALS: 1 piece of white paper per child, crayons, pencils

DIRECTIONS
1. Let each child draw a picture of what he or she is thankful for.

2. Stand in a circle.

3. Go around the circle, letting each child have a turn.

Leader: Thanks be to God for all our blessings.

(Have the first child show his/her picture and tell what it is.)

Child 1: Thanks be to God for music and flutes.

Children: Thank you, God, for music and flutes!

Leader: Thanks be to God for all our blessings.

Child 2: Thanks be to God for school and teachers.

Children: Thank you, God, for school and teachers.

Leader: Thanks be to God for all our blessings.

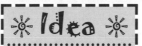

See pages 25-26 for Thanksgiving calls to worship, page 100 for Thanksgiving benedictions, and page 134 for "Thanks Be to God." See worship service "Give Thanks and Share, page 158."

Finish by saying:

Leader: Thanks be to God for our blessings!

Children: Thanks be to God for our blessings!

Leader: Let's thank God for *(points to each picture)*

Children: Music and flutes, school and teachers, trumpets and band.

Everyone: THANKS BE TO GOD! THANKS BE TO GOD!

(Let the children jump up and clap their hands.)

GIVE THANKS TO GOD

 Scripture: Psalm 106:1

 (Sung to "Frere Jacques")

Give thanks to God!
Give thanks to God!
Who is good!
Who is good!
God's love endures forever!
God's love endures forever!
Amen.
Amen.

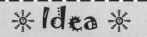

Try these other verses:
For our food.
It helps us grow strong.
For our homes.
They keep us warm and safe.
For our friends.
They are fun to play with.
For our families.
They will always love us.

IF YOU WANT TO GIVE THANKS

 Scripture: Psalm 47:1

 (Sung to "If You're Happy")

If you want to give
thanks, clap your
hands. (clap, clap)
If you want to give
thanks, clap your
hands. (clap, clap)
If you want to give
thanks, if you want
to give thanks, if
you want to give thanks,
Clap your hands!
(clap, clap)

☀ **Ideas** ☀

Try these movements:
 Stamp your feet
 Click your tongue
 Nod your head
 Shout "Thank You!"

To challenge older kids try this:
 Clap and stamp
 Click your tongue,
 nod your head
 (click and nod)

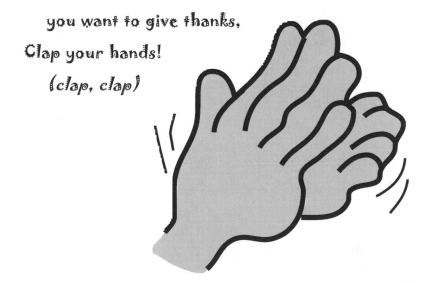

GLORY TO GOD IN THE HIGHEST

 Scripture: Luke 2:10-14

Share the Christmas story with the children.

Thank you God, for sending us Jesus. Help us to love Jesus and follow his ways. Help us to accept Jesus as the Lord and Savior of our lives. Let us bring Jesus the gift of our love. GLORIA, GLORIA, GLORIA! GLORY TO GOD IN THE HIGHEST! AMEN!

WELCOME, JESUS

 Scripture: Luke 2:10-14

Share the Christmas story with the children.

Leader: Let us welcome Jesus into our hearts.

Children: Welcome, Jesus!

Leader: Let us accept Jesus as our Savior.

Children: Welcome, Jesus!

Leader: Thank you God for sending us your Son, a Savior who is Christ the Lord.

Children: Welcome, Jesus!

All: AMEN!

☀ **Ideas** ☀

1. See pages 30-31 for calls to worship and page 104 for Christmas benedictions.
2. Combine with "It's a Baby Boy" on pages 137-38 and "Happy Birthday, Jesus!" on page 138.

GLORY TO GOD

 Scripture: Luke 2:10-14

Share the Christmas story with the children.

 (Sung to "Row, Row, Row Your Boat")

Glory, glory, glory to God,

In the highest heaven!

Peace on earth,

Goodwill to all.

Glory, Gloria!

LET'S ALL SING A SONG

 Scripture: Luke 2:10-14

Share the Christmas story with the children.

 (Sung to "Pop! Goes the Weasel")

Let's all sing a song!

Glory to God in the highest!

Peace on earth,

Goodwill to all.

Glory to God in the

highest!

 SOMETHING SPECIAL

The books *Piggyback Songs in Praise of God* and *Piggyback Songs in Praise of Jesus* compiled by Jean Warren have more songs to sing with children.

There are several words hidden along the letter path. Each word spells out something we can do to praise the Lord. Circle each word. Print the leftover letters in the spaces to answer the question.

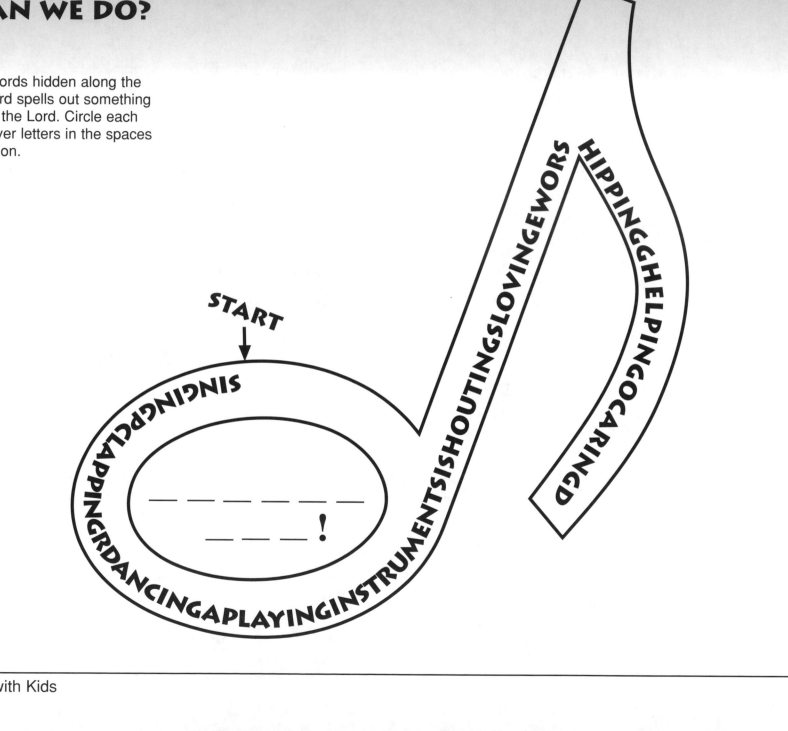

PUZZLE:
WHEN WE PRAY

Color   R: Red   B: Blue
G: Green

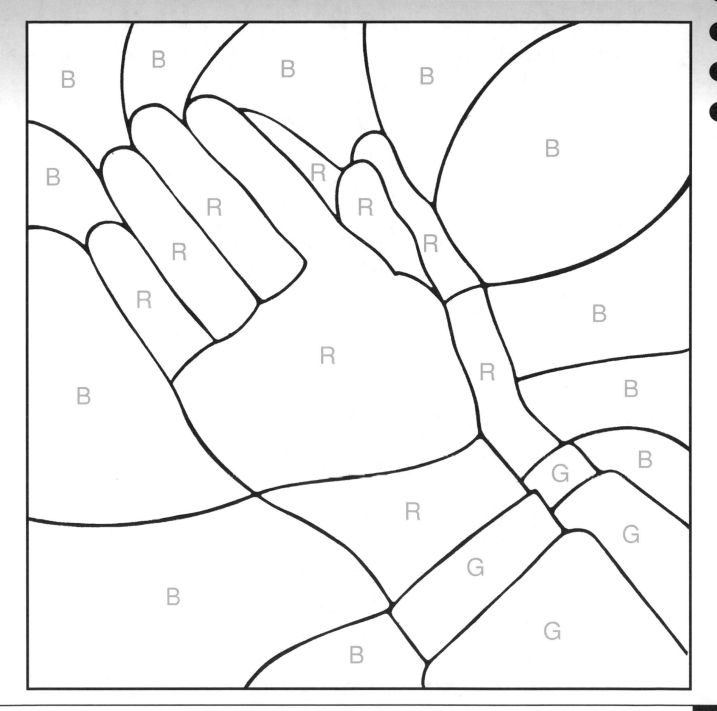

PRAYER BEAR

 Scripture: 1 Thessalonians 5:25

MATERIALS: 1 soft, cuddly stuffed teddy bear; tape of soothing, instrumental music; audio cassette player

DIRECTIONS

1. Darken the room. Play the tape.

2. Sit in a circle with the children.

3. Holding the bear, the leader begins by making a prayer request. Pray for friends, family, concerns, joys, and so on.

5. Pass the bear to the child on the right, who adds a sentence to the prayer request.

6. Go all the way around the circle.

Idea

Substitute other items for the bear.

Hint

Help children think of sentences to say.

BUBBLE PRAYERS

 Scripture: Proverbs 28:20

MATERIALS: 1 jar of bubble liquid with wand

Tell the children that God gives us many blessings. Blow some bubbles. Tell the children: **"God gives us even more blessings than there are bubbles in this jar."** You can also look at the rainbows in the bubbles. Talk about the rainbow in Noah's Ark. What did that rainbow mean?

DIRECTIONS

1. Sit in a circle with the children, and begin a group prayer.

2. Let each child have a turn blowing bubbles.

3. Before the bubbles burst, the child must add something to your group prayer.

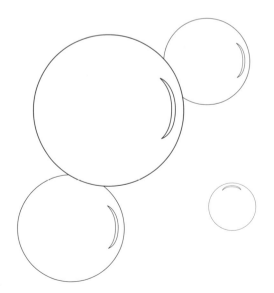

Hints

1. Hold the jar of bubbles for younger children or those who have motor difficulties.
2. Some children may need help in blowing bubbles.
3. Help younger children think of prayers to add.

ART: BURSTING WITH PRAYERS

Write a prayer inside each bubble. You can write a prayer for family members, friends, yourself, or things that are happening in our world. Color the bubbles.

PLAY BALL

Scripture: Psalm 109:26

MATERIALS: 1 round plastic or foam ball, index cards, pencils

PREPARATION

1. Give each child an index card and a pencil.

2. Ask the children to print prayer requests on the cards (examples: Do well on a test, be more honest, help Grandma get well soon). Have children print their names on the cards.

3. Collect the cards.

DIRECTIONS

1. Sit in a circle with the children.

2. Take the first card from the pack of prayer requests.

3. Roll the ball to that child. As the ball is rolling say a prayer for that child. (example: Help (child's name) do well on her math test.)

4. When the child receives the ball, he or she can say: "Help me, O Lord, my God."

5. The child rolls the ball back to the leader.

6. Repeat until all children have had a turn.

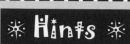 **Hints**

1. You may need to give children ideas for their prayers. Do you have a test this week? Do you know someone who is sick you'd like to pray for?

2. Let younger children dictate their requests. Print their requests on the cards for them.

BOUNCE IT!

Scripture: Psalm 150:1

This is an enjoyable way for you and the children to greet one another as you gather for your time together.

MATERIALS: 1 large plastic ball that bounces well

DIRECTIONS

1. Stand in a circle with the children.

2. As you bounce the ball to one child, say: "Thank you, God, for sending (child's name) to us today!"

3. The child catches the ball. All of the children shout, "PRAISE THE LORD FOR (child's name)."

4. The child bounces the ball to another child and says, "Thank you, God, for sending (child's name) to us today!"

5. The child catches the ball. All the children shout, "PRAISE THE LORD FOR (child's name)!"

6. Continue until all children have had a turn.

 **Hint**

Very young children might find it easier to roll the ball to one another.

 **Ideas**

1. Talk about the things the children chose to praise God for. Why should we appreciate these things?

2. Sing "Please Be with Us" on page 72.

 VARIATIONS

Let the children think of things to praise God for (examples: sunshine, worms).

ART: CATCH A PRAYER

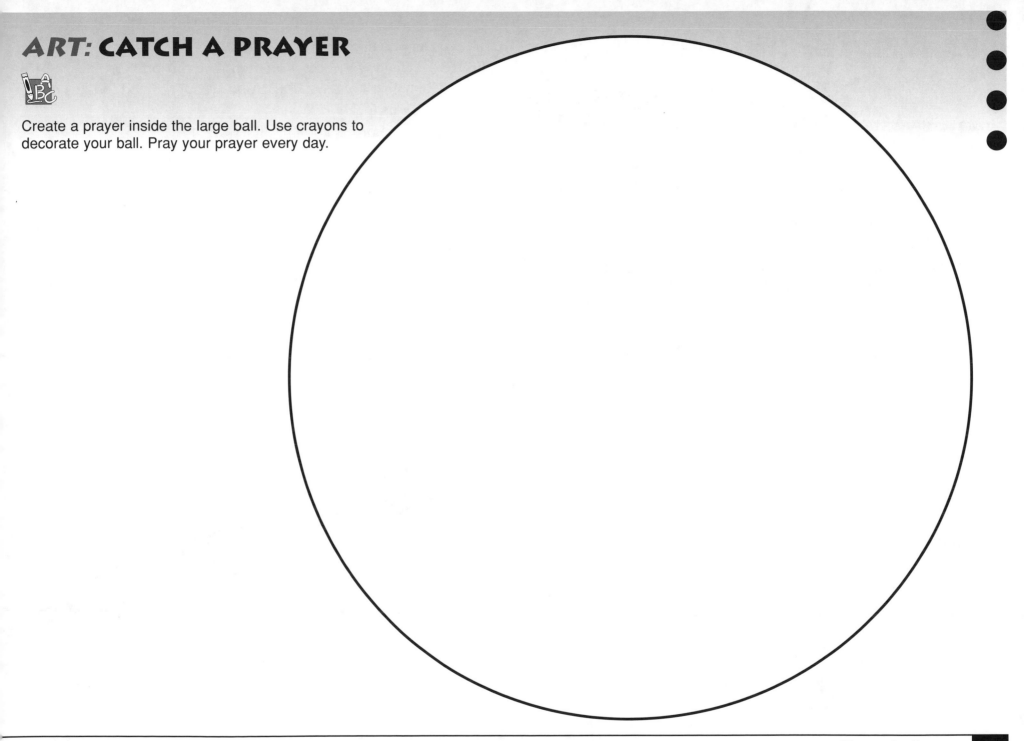

Create a prayer inside the large ball. Use crayons to decorate your ball. Pray your prayer every day.

PRAYER CHAINS

 Scripture: Psalm 145:9

MATERIALS: 1 pastel colored strip of paper per child, 1 pencil per child, stapler and staples

DIRECTIONS

1. Give each child a colored strip of paper and a pencil.

2. Tell the children to print a prayer request and their name on the strip of paper The leader also prints a prayer request.

3. Staple the strips of paper into a paper chain.

4. Sit in a circle with the children.

5. The leader removes the first link of the chain and prays for the child whose name is on the link.

6. The leader passes the chain to the child on the right, who removes a link and prays for the child whose name is on the link. Go around the entire circle.

Example:

Leader: Please be with (child's name) and his family as they travel to visit his aunt and uncle. Let them have a good time and bring them safely home to us.

Children: The Lord is good to all.

Child 1: Please be with Valerie's friend Katie who broke her arm. Help her arm heal fast.

Children: The Lord is good to all.

✳ Hint ✳

To adapt this for young children, ask each child to share a prayer request. Help them think of something to pray for. Print the request on a strip of paper. Link these together to form a chain. Each child can pull off a link and give it to the leader. The leader will make the prayer request. The children can respond with: THANK YOU, GOD.

To end the prayer:

Leader: Thank you God for listening to our prayers. Please be with all of us and all those we mentioned today. Let all of us feel your love.

All: The Lord is good to all. AMEN!

✦ VARIATIONS

1. Have each child make their own prayer chain. Each child can write seven requests for their chain.

2. The children can take their chains home. Each day the child can remove a link and pray that request.

3. Send home a note to parents, explaining the prayer chain. Encourage families to pray together for these requests.

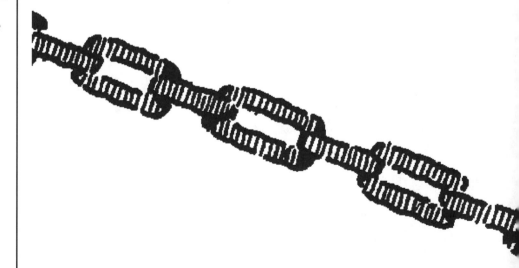

GIVE ME A HAND

 Scripture: Psalm 47:1

MATERIALS: One handprint per child
(Copy these on a variety of pastel colors.),
one pencil per child, tape

☀ Idea ☀

Sing "Lord Hear Us"
on page 72.

DIRECTIONS

1. Give each child a hand print and a
   pencil.
2. Let the children write prayers on their handprints.
3. Tape the handprints together with the prayers showing. Hang
   them where they can be seen.
4. Create a prayer based on what is written on the handprints.
5. Use the scripture verse as the children's response.

☀ Hints ☀

1. Use your hand as a pattern for the print.

2. Help younger children and those who have difficulty printing.

3. Some children will need help thinking of prayers.

ART: HANDS OF PRAYER

 Have the children lay their hands on a sheet of paper. Ask
someone to trace around them. Write a prayer inside each
hand. Pray that prayer every day.

PRAYER VINE

Scripture: John 15:5

MATERIALS: white trellis (available at garden stores), brown construction paper, green construction paper (autumn colors in autumn), leaf pattern (trace a large leaf), pencils, tape

PREPARATION:
1. Use the brown construction paper to make a large vine.

2. Attach the vine to the trellis.

3. Prop the trellis against a wall.

DIRECTIONS
1. Give each child a paper leaf.

2. Have the children print prayer requests and their names on the leaves.

3. As each child puts their leaf on the vine, have them share their prayer request.

4. The next time your group meets, ask each child to share what happened with their prayer request. As requests are fulfilled, remove the leaves.

5. Children can add a new leaf at each meeting.

 VARIATIONS

1. Put the leaves into a basket. Let each child pull out one leaf and read the request aloud. Offer a prayer for that request, and put the leaf on the vine. During each meeting check with the children to discover how the requests turned out.

2. Give each child a leaf with a classmate's name written on it. Let each child write something affirming about that child on the leaf. Read the affirmations aloud. Let the children put the leaves on the vine.

3. Let the children think of ways they can do God's work in the world (examples: helping others, being kind to people, doing extra chores at home). Let the children write one idea per leaf, sign their name, and put it on the vine.

4. Put the names of friends, family, or church members on the leaves. Use one leaf per person. Hang them on the vine.

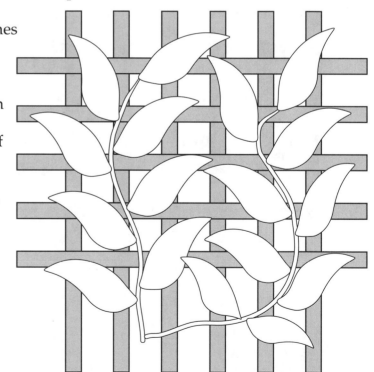

ART:
A VINE OF BLESSINGS

Write a blessing inside each leaf. Thank God for each of these blessings. It may take several days or even several weeks to fill in all of the leaves. Each time you fill in a leaf, color it light green.

Chapter 4: Benedictions

The word *benediction* means "good words," and it is used to close the worship service.

When people come to worship God, they may be feeling frightened, angry, worried, or sad. Hopefully, by the end of the worship service they will feel comforted by God's love. We speak and sing benedictions to remind people that God loves and cares for us. It is an "extra" prayer we offer to one another.

The spoken and musical benedictions included here can be "mixed and matched" as you choose.

KNOW THAT I AM WITH YOU

 Scripture: Genesis 28:15

God, Go with Us
God, go with us this week. Help us to show your love for us with everyone we meet. AMEN.

God, Help Us
God, help us be forgiving and loving toward one another. Thank you for staying with us. AMEN.

God, Be with Us
God, be with us. Let us be kind to all we meet. Help us to remember to do the best we can in all we do. AMEN.

Thank You, God
Thank you, God, for another new week, a week filled with unknown events and happenings.
Help us to remember to live our lives as you want us to. AMEN.

Be with Us
Be with us, God, as we go into the world. We promise to try to let everyone we meet
know of all of the good things you do for us. AMEN.

Joyful Praise
God, let us praise you joyfully this week. Let us praise you with the words we
speak and the things we do. Thank you for always watching over us. AMEN.

We Are Not Alone
Let us praise you, God, in all we do. Help us to remember that we are not alone
and that you are with us. AMEN.

Loving God
Loving God, let us show our love for you. Help us to show our love for other people,
for our families, for our teachers and for our friends. Thank you for being our guide. AMEN.

Creator God
Creator God, be with us as we go through this week. There will be challenges for all of us. Give us the strength we need to face those
challenges. Help us do the best we can do all week. In your name we pray. AMEN.

Love of God
Thank you for all of the love you have for us God. Help us to be kind and thoughtful. Help us do our best in school. Help us to play
nicely with others. Be with us and let us do the best we can. In the name of the Creator, Christ, and Living Spirit. AMEN.

GOD, BE GRACIOUS

 Scripture: Psalm 67:1

 (Sung to "Michael, Row the Boat Ashore")

God be gracious unto you and bless you.
God be gracious unto you and bless you.

We will sing to God with joy and gladness.
We will sing to God with joy and gladness.

We go now on our way, please go with us.
We go now on our way, please go with us.

I WILL PRAISE YOU

 Scripture: Psalm 86:12

 (Sung to "Frere Jacques")

I will praise you!
I will praise you!
Every day.
Every day.
And I'll glorify you!
And I'll glorify you!
Forever!
Forever!

GOD'S LOVE ENDURES FOREVER

 Scripture: Psalm 106:1

 (Sung to "Michael, Row the Boat Ashore")

God's love endures forever, Alleluia.
Go forth and share God's love, Alleluia.

SING TO THE LORD A NEW SONG

 Scripture: Psalm 96:1

 (Sung to "Skip to My Lou")

Sing to the Lord a new song.
Sing to the Lord a new song.
Sing to the Lord a new song,
And praise God's holy name!

Declare God's glory to everyone.
Declare God's glory to everyone.
Declare God's glory to everyone,
To everyone you meet!

Worship the Lord in all you do.
Worship the Lord in all you do.
Worship the Lord in all you do,
As you go forth this week!

GOD WILL WATCH YOU

 Scripture: Matthew 28:20

 (Sung to "Frere Jacques")

God is with you,
God is with you,
And will watch you,
And will watch you,
Wherever you go.
Wherever you go.
God is with you.
God is with you.

GOD WILL GO WITH YOU

 Scripture: Exodus 33:14

 (Sung to "Michael, Row the Boat Ashore")

God will go with you, Alleluia.
God will give you rest, Alleluia.

GO INTO THE WORLD

 Scripture: Mark 16:15

 (Sung to "Skip to My Lou")

Go into the world proclaiming love.
Go into the world proclaiming love.

Go into the world proclaiming love,
The love of God the Father (Creator)!

Go into the world proclaiming love.
Go into the world proclaiming love.
Go into the world proclaiming love,
The love of Jesus Christ!

Go into the world proclaiming love.
Go into the world proclaiming love.
Go into the world proclaiming love,
The love of the Living Spirit!

GOD IS ALWAYS WITH YOU

 Scripture: Genesis 28:15

 (Sung to "The Bear Went Over the Mountain")

God is always with you.
God is always with you.
God is always with you,
Everywhere you go!
Everywhere you go!
Everywhere you go!
God is always with you!
God is always with you!
God is always with you!
Everywhere you go!

PUZZLE: WHAT ARE YOU SAYING?

A=1; B=2; C=3; D=4; E=5; F=6; G=7; H=8; I=9; J=10; K=11; L=12; M=13; N=14; O=15; P=16; Q=17; R=18; S=19; T=20; U=21; V=22; W=23; X=24; Y=25; Z=26.

 Use the code above to decipher the code.

```
___ ___ ___   ___ ___ ___ ___   ___ ___ ___ ___ ___
20  8   5     12  15  18  4     2   12  5   19  19

___ ___ ___   ___ ___ ___   ___ ___ ___ ___   ___ ___ ___
25  15  21    1   14  4      11  5   5   16    25  15  21

___ ___ ___   ___ ___ ___ ___   ___ ___ ___ ___   ___ ___ ___
20  8   5     12  15  18  4     13  1   11  5     8   9   19

___ ___ ___ ___   ___ ___   ___ ___ ___ ___ ___
6   1   3   5     20  15    19  8   9   14  5

___ ___ ___ ___   ___ ___ ___   ___ ___ ___   ___ ___
21  16  15  14    25  15  21    1   14  4      2   5

___ ___ ___ ___ ___ ___ ___ ___   ___ ___   ___ ___ ___
7   18  1   3   9   15  21  19    20  15    25  15  21

___ ___ ___   ___ ___ ___ ___   ___ ___ ___ ___   ___ ___
20  8   5     12  15  18  4     12  9   6   20    21  16

___ ___ ___   ___ ___ ___ ___ ___ ___ ___ ___ ___ ___ ___
8   9   19    3   15  21  14  20  5   14  1   14  3   5

___ ___ ___ ___   ___ ___ ___   ___ ___ ___   ___ ___ ___ ___
21  16  15  14    25  15  21    1   14  4      7   9   22  5

___ ___ ___   ___ ___ ___ ___ ___.
25  15  21    16  5   1   3   5

___ ___ ___ ___ ___ ___ ___ 6:24-26
14  21  13  2   5   18  19
```

BAPTISM

 Scripture: Matthew 28:19

Dear God, thank you for the gift of life. Help us remember we are baptized in your love. Let us share that love with everyone we meet. AMEN.

WE ARE BAPTIZED WITH LOVE

 Scripture: Mark 1:8

 (Sung to "Michael, Row the Boat Ashore")

We are baptized
with love, Alleluia.
In the name of
God, Christ,
and Spirit.

PUZZLE:
WE ARE BAPTIZED

Unscramble the words in the cross. The circled letters fit into the spaces at the bottom of the cross to spell a special word.

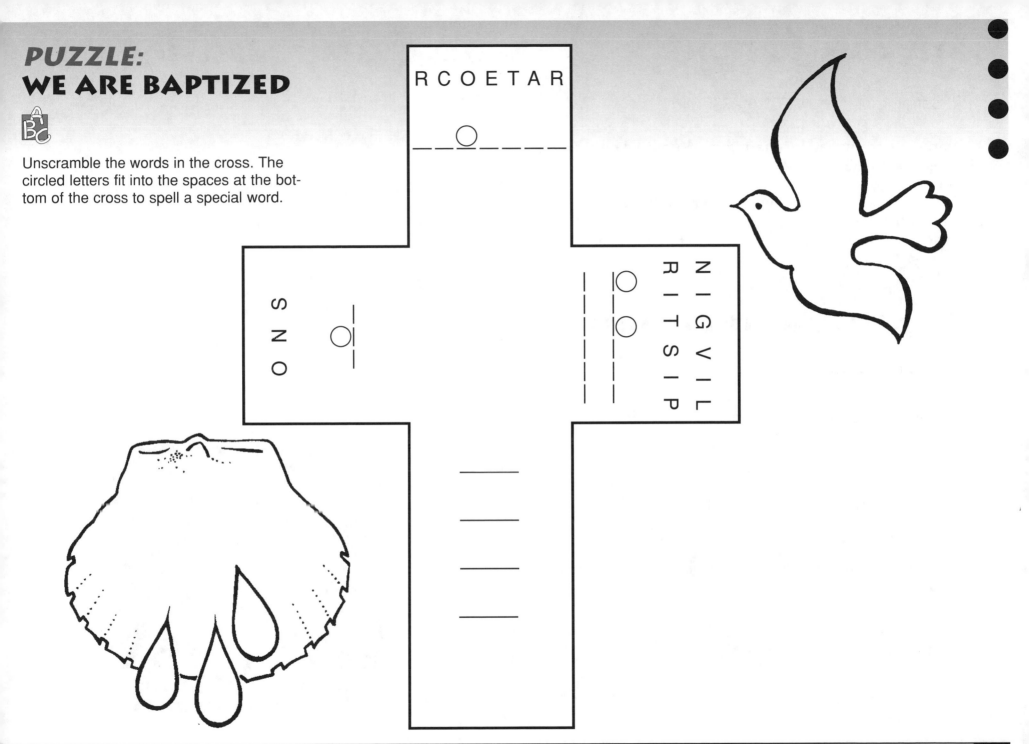

R C O E T A R

_ _ _ O _ _ _ _

O N S

_ O _

N I G V I L
R I T S I P

_ _ _ _ _ O _ _
_ _ _ _ O _

_ _ _ _ _

HOLY COMMUNION

 Scripture: Matthew 26:26-27

Dear Jesus, thank you for sharing such a special meal with us. Help us to remember that you died to save us from our sins. Amen.

Help us, Jesus, to live our lives as you want us to. Let us remember that you shared this meal with us to give us strength to do your work in the world. Help us to forgive others as you forgive us. Amen.

GO AND SHARE THE GOOD NEWS

 Scripture: Mark 16:15

(Sung to "Clementine")

Go and share
the good news
About Jesus Christ.
Let the world know
of his glory,
That he died to
save us all.

SHARE CHRIST'S BLESSINGS

 Scripture: Mark 16:15

 (Sung to "Frere Jacques")

Share Christ's blessings,
Share Christ's blessings,
With your friends.
With your friends.
Let them know Christ died for us.
Let them know Christ died for us.
Amen.
Amen.

PUZZLE: WHO ARE WE?

Unscramble the names.

TEREP   ⃝ __ __ __ __ __

MAJES   __ ☐ __ __ __

NHOJ   __ ☐ __ __

DREWAN   __ __ ⃝ __ __ __

LIPHIP   ☐ __ __ __ ☐ ⃝ __

MEWTHOOLRAB   __ __ __ __ __ __ ⃝ __ __ __ __ __

HATMTEW   __ __ __ __ ☐ __ __

MASTOH   __ __ __ __ ⃝ __

SEMJA   __ __ __ ☐ __

SADEUTHD   ☐ __ __ __ __ ⃝ __ ☐ __

ISMNO   __ ⃝ __ __ __

ADJSU   __ __ __ __ ⃝ __

Print the circled letters here. _____

Print the squared letters here. _____

Unscramble both sets of letters to fill in the blanks.

These men were the __ __ __ C __ __ __ __ of Jesus Christ. They were also called the twelve __ __ __ __ __ __ __ __ __.

BLESSED IS HE

 Scripture: Matthew 21:9

Blessed is he who comes in the name of the Lord.
Help us to share Christ's blessings with everyone we meet this week. Hosanna! AMEN.

LET US TELL THE WORLD

 Scripture: Matthew 21:9

Hosanna! Let us tell the world about Christ and what he has done for us. AMEN.

SHOUT HOSANNA

 Scripture: Mark 11:9

 (Sung to "Mary Had a Little Lamb")

Shout Hosanna, tell the world, tell the world, tell the world.
Shout Hosanna, tell the world all about the Lord!

HOSANNA, TO GOD IN THE HIGHEST

 Scripture: Matthew 21:9

 (Sung to "Skip to My Lou")

Hosanna! Sing Hosanna!
Hosanna! Sing Hosanna!
Hosanna! Sing Hosanna!
Sing to the Lord!

PUZZLE:
WHAT DID YOU SAY?

Color: Y: Yellow R: Red
O: Orange G: Green
B: Blue P: Purple
K: Pink

GLAD EASTER

 Scripture: Mark 16:15

Praise the Lord! Christ has risen! Let us go and share this wonderful news! Amen!

God, what wonderful news we have heard this morning! Christ has risen and lives forever. Alleluia! Amen!

GO TELL THE WORLD

 Scripture: Mark 16:15

 (Sung to "Wheels on the Bus")

Go tell the world that Christ is risen,
Christ is risen, Christ is risen!
Go tell the world that Christ is risen.
Tell everyone you meet!

Tell them Christ died to save us, died to save us,
died to save us.
Tell that Christ died to save us, from all our sins.
(Repeat first stanza)

CHRIST AROSE ON EASTER MORNING

 Scripture: Mark 16:15

 (Sung to "London Bridge")

Christ arose on Easter morning, Easter morning,
Easter morning.

Christ arose on Easter morning.
Go and spread the word!

THANKSGIVING BLESSINGS

 Scripture: Psalm 9:1

Creator God, thank you for this wonderful and beautiful world that you have created for us. Help us to care for it with love and concern. Thank you, God! Amen!

Thank you, God, for everything you give us. Thank you for our homes, our food, our schools, our families, our pets, toys, and friends. Most of all thank you for your love for us. Help us to share that love with all we meet. Amen.

GIVE THANKS FOR ALL OF YOUR BLESSINGS

 Scripture: Psalm 9:1-2

 (Sung to " The Bear Went Over the Mountain")

Give thanks for all of your blessings.
Give thanks for all of your blessings.
Give thanks for all of your blessings,
And go and spread the word.
Tell all about our Lord!
Tell all about our Lord!
Go into the world now.
Go into the world now.
Go into the world now.
And give your thanks to God.

PUZZLE:
WHAT AM I?

Color: B: Brown G: Green
R: Red Y: Yellow

Write a blessing inside each feather. Color each feather any color you choose.

JESUS' BIRTHDAY

 Scripture: Micah 7:7

Jesus' birthday is coming in _____ (4, 3, 2, 1) more week(s). What wonderful news! We're really excited! God, it's hard to wait. Help us to wait patiently for Christmas. Help us to wait patiently for all the gifts we will give and receive. Help us to remember that Jesus is God's gift to us. Thank you, God! AMEN!

HELP US TO REMEMBER

 Scripture: Micah 7:7

Dear God, help us to prepare for your Son's birth. Help us to remember to share with people who don't have all of the things that we have. Help us to be loving and kind to each other. Help us to remember to bring our gifts of love and joy to Christ. Let us remember to share this good news with the world. AMEN!

TELL THE WORLD

 Scripture: Micah 7:7

 (Sung to "London Bridge")

Tell the world that Jesus' birthday,

Jesus' birthday, Jesus' birthday

Tell the world it's coming.

In only four more weeks!

IT WILL BE HERE VERY SOON

 Scripture: Micah 7:7

 (Sung to "Mary Had a Little Lamb")

It will be here very soon, very soon, very soon.

It will be here very soon.

It's only four more weeks!

Four more weeks till Jesus' birthday,

Jesus' birthday, Jesus' birthday!

Four more weeks till Jesus' birthday!

It's only four more weeks!

[Change number of weeks each week.]

PUZZLE:
HOW LONG?

Color one square each week of Advent. What does the picture tell you?

Color: Y: Yellow   O: Orange
G: Green   B: Blue
P: Purple   K: Pink

BLESSED CHRISTMAS

 Scripture: Luke 2:10-11

God, it's just as you promised. A new baby was born in Bethlehem. Angels and shepherds came to welcome him and praise him. Let us praise Jesus every day of our lives, by sharing his love with one another. Amen.

A WONDERFUL GIFT

 Scripture: Luke 2:10-11

Gracious God, thank you for sending us your son. What a wonderful gift you have given to us. Help us share Christ's gift of love with everyone we meet. Amen.

CHRIST WAS BORN

 Scripture: Luke 2:10-11

 (Sung to "Clementine")

Christ was born.

Christ was born.

Christ was born, in Bethlehem.

Christ was born.

Christ was born.

Go now, and tell the world!

CHRIST WAS BORN IN BETHLEHEM

 Scripture: Luke 2:10-11

 (Sung to "London Bridge")

Christ was born on Christmas Eve, Christmas Eve,
Christmas Eve.
Christ was born on Christmas Eve,
Long, long ago!

Christ came to save us from our sins, from our sins,
from our sins.
Christ came to save us from our sins,
Long, long ago!

Go tell the world that Jesus came, Jesus came, Jesus came.
Go tell the world that Jesus came,
To save us from our sins!

PUZZLE:
WHAT'S THAT IN THE SKY?

Color: Y: Yellow   B: Dark Blue

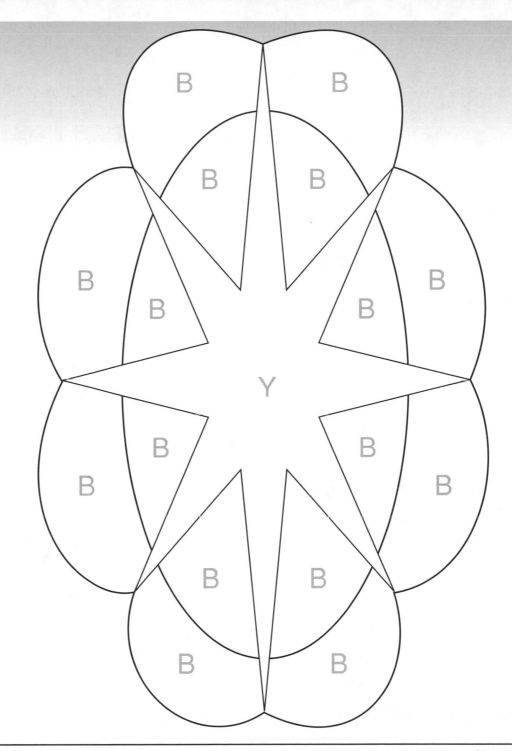

EPIPHANY

 Scripture: Matthew 2:10-11

Loving God, that was a long journey those Wise Men made to see Jesus. What wonderful gifts they brought to him. Help us to follow the star just like the Wise Men did. Help us to follow Christ's teachings. AMEN.

BRIGHT SHINING STAR

 Scripture: Matthew 2:10-11

Dear God, thank you for a beautiful and bright shining star that led the Wise Men to Jesus. Help us to be brave just like they were. Help us to keep following the light of the star so we will always be following Jesus. Help us to share the gift of love that Christ gives to us. In your name we pray, AMEN.

GO FORTH AND SHARE

 Scripture: Matthew 2:10-11

 (Sung to "This Is the Way We Wash Our Clothes")

Go forth and share the gift of love,
the gift of love, the gift of love.
Go forth and share the gift of love,
that Christ has come to give us.

SHARE YOUR GIFTS

 Scripture: Matthew 2:10-11

 (Sung to "Brahms's Lullaby")

Go forth, share your gifts,
Share your gifts with all.
Share the love of Jesus Christ,
Who came to save us all.
Praise the Lord.
And tell the world,
That Christ came for us.
Share the love and the peace,
That comes from Christ.

PUZZLE: WHAT DID THEY RIDE?

Color: B: Brown G: Green
Y: Yellow U: Blue

Part 2: WORSHIP TALKS

"Let the little children come to me; do not stop them; for it is to such as these that the kingdom of God belongs." (Mark 10:14)

Many churches offer within their worship service a special time for the children. Usually, the pastor or another adult presents a short message for the children. In many churches, the children, ranging in age from three to ten, are invited to sit or stand with pastor or worship leader in a designated area of the sanctuary.

This section includes many different stories and ideas that can be used for children's worship talks. Each talk includes a suggested Bible verse. Share this verse with the children. Discuss what the verse means and relate the lesson to that particular verse.

Stories and other activities provide an interesting means of communicating beliefs with children. In preparing worship talks, be creative in your use of materials and stories. Bible stories, personal experience stories, and original stories are included here. Other stories that reflect Christian themes can also be used. When preparing talks for children it is important to provide examples that they experience and relate to. Messages need to be concrete rather than abstract.

Jesus was a storyteller. He used stories to teach Christian principles to people. He made use of personal experience stories and created many original stories to help people learn about God. We can do that today.

When using stories with children, take time to discuss them by sharing your thoughts and encouraging the children to share their ideas as well. However, keep in mind that some stories are so beautiful, they can stand alone and need no discussion. Read or tell the story and allow the children to "take what they need with them."

These worship talks can be used as a part of a congregational worship service, children's church, a Bible lesson, children's choir, or other children's ministry time.

The stories listed under "Something Special" can become part of a suggested worship talk. The songs suggested can be sung by the children or by your children's choir.

Now, let the children come, and share your love of the Lord with them.

Hints for offering worship talks within adult worship

1. If you have never used a children's sermon (worship talk) as part of your worship service, try it. Begin gradually. Offer a worship talk for children once a month. This allows the congregation to get used to it gradually. Over time, phase it in so you have a children's time each week. Soon the congregation will look forward to these times. Remind people that Jesus said, "Let the children come." Keep in mind that children are our future. We want them to feel welcome in church now so they will continue to attend once they become adults.

2. Make the worship talk interesting for children and adults. Adults can and do learn to appreciate the lessons taught in these times. Over time, you will find the adults do listen and learn.

3. Invite different members who are good with children to offer worship talks. Children's librarians who do story times can present outstanding and enjoyable experiences. If you have professional storytellers in your midst, encourage them to offer a worship talk. Teachers can also be asked. Because these people know how to keep children's attention, they are a good choice for offering worship talks.

4. Including adult members of the congregation in a worship talk can and does provide a rewarding experience for all.

5. Asking parents to assist helps children learn that they are valuable to their parents. (See: "Will You Still Love Me?" page 149)

6. Asking adults to help, encourages everyone to be attentive. It also helps them to feel they are contributing to the well-being of our children. (See "Come Be Baptized," page 141)

Chapter 5: All About Me

The messages in this section will help children understand that they were created in God's image. Each of them is a special and unique creation. God's image is good, therefore we all are good and special in God's eyes. These talks will also help them understand that God needs all of us to help do the Lord's work. Even children can help God. Through these talks, children will learn about accepting people who are different and who have different viewpoints. Children will learn that there are values God wants us to have.

YOU ARE SPECIAL

Scripture: Genesis 1:26-27

PROPS: A paper bag with a wig in a color and style completely different from your own hair.

Say: **I am really tired of how I look. I wanted my hair to be different, so I went to the store and bought this.** *(Pull the wig out of the bag and put it on your head.)* Be prepared for some interesting reactions. The children may not know what to say, which is fine.

Ask: **Do you like my hair this way or do you like it the way it was?"** (Hopefully, they will say they like your own hair better.) *Remove the wig.* Say: **God gave me ____ (color) hair and ___ (color) eyes because God knew that is what would look best on me. God gave ____(name) ____(color) eyes and ____(color) hair because God knew that is what would look best on her/him.**

　　God created each of us to look different because that is one way God has of showing each of us is special. If you have a set of identical twins, explain that even though they look alike, there are some differences in them. Ask their parents beforehand to share how they tell the twins apart. Remind the children that God loves each of us so much, that we are created to be very special and unique.

· ·

SOMETHING SPECIAL

Some Stories to share:
The Mixed-Up Chameleon
by Eric Carle
A Color of His Own by Leo Lionni
(Give each child an outline of a chameleon to take home and color "in your very own way.")
You Look Ridiculous, Said the Rhinoceros to the Hippopotamus by Bernard Waber

> ☀ **Idea** ☀
> · · · · · · · · · · · · · · · · · ·
> Use the books or make these stories into flannel board stories.

· ·

PUZZLE: GOD THINKS I'M SPECIAL

Draw your face and hair on this blank face.

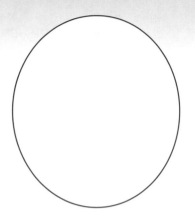

Decode this message.

A=1; B=2; C=3; D=4; E=5; F=6; G=7; H=8; I=9; J=10; K=11; L=12;

M=13; N=14; O=15; P=16; Q=17; R=18; S=19; T-20; U=21; V=22;

W=23; X=24; Y=25; Z=26

___ ___ ___ ___ ___ ___ ___ ___ ___
7　15　4　13　1　4　5　13　5

___ ___ ___ ___ ___ ___ ___.
19　16　5　3　9　1　12

On the back of this paper, write things that make you special. Ask your parents to tell you why you are special to them.

UNDER CONSTRUCTION

Scripture: 2 Peter 3:18

PROPS: A variety of building materials (blocks, Legos, Lincoln Logs, straws, cards, string, yarn, and so forth), a set of blueprints, an instruction manual (for a VCR, TV, and so forth), Bible

TAKE-HOME GIFTS: Cards with Bible verses written on them (one per child) (for example, Exodus 20:12; Exodus 20:15; Matthew 7:12; Matthew 22:37-39)

Place all of the materials on the floor. Ask several children to construct something unique. Let them work for a few minutes, and then ask them to stop.

Talk about how difficult it is to construct a home. It takes many people, and it is very hard work. Even after the home is finished, the people who live in it have to work hard to care for it.

Say: **Our growth is hard work too. We are always growing and changing, even after we become adults. It is a lot of hard work for parents to raise a child. It's hard to know just what to do sometimes.**

Ask the children if they think it is difficult to know what decisions to make about things or if it is difficult to know what is the right thing to do. Tell them adults feel that way too. Explain that we are always growing and learning, even after we become adults.

Show them the set of blueprints, and ask if they know what they are and what they are used for. (They tell the builders how to construct a building.)

Say: **All of the directions to build a house are in these blueprints. They helped the builders know how to construct it correctly.** Show them the instruction manual, and ask them to tell you why you would need it. (So I know how to use my ___.)

Say: **God has given us a set of blueprints that tells us how to live our lives. Do you know what it is called?** (The Bible)

Bring out your Bible, and open it to The Ten Commandments. Say: **Look, here are The Ten Commandments. They tell us what to do and what not to do. Sometimes we aren't sure what to do. Let's say you are in the store with a friend, and that friend wants you to steal some toys. You aren't real sure about doing that. Look here, look what it says, "Do not steal." Is it okay if you and your friend steal the toys?** (no) Ask: **Why not?** (Let them explain in their own words.) Share others if you wish.

Point to the construction materials and explain that we need directions that tell us how to put things together. We use blueprints or instruction manuals. We also need directions that tell us how to live as good Christians, and we use our ____? (Bibles).

Give each child a card with a Bible verse written on it, and tell them to take it home and look it up with their parents to see what it says. They can put the Bible verse on their bulletin board so they remember to use their Bibles to help them live as good Christians.

• •

 SOMETHING SPECIAL

A Song to Sing:
"Kids Under Construction" by Bill and Gloria Gaither in *Sing 'n' Celebrate for Kids*, vol. 2

Have the children sing this the day you present this worship talk.

GOD NEEDS ME

Scripture: Psalm 100:2

PROPS: Pictures of children doing things. (for example, helping others, hugging, playing)

TAKE-HOME GIFT: one large "Super Kids" or "Number 1" sticker per child

Ask: **Do you need your parents? Why?** (Let them share their thoughts.)

Ask: **Does anybody need you?** (Let them share their thoughts.)

Show the pictures to the children. Ask them to tell you what is happening in each picture.

Explain that God put each of us here on earth for a purpose. We need our parents to take care of us. We need teachers to help us learn all the things we need to know. We need pastors at church to help us learn about God. We need the choir to provide special music for us each week.

Say: **God needs you too. God needs you to show love for others. God needs you to help others.**

Ask: **How can you help other children at school? How can you help your friends? How can you help at home?** After everyone has shared their thoughts, remind them that God loves them. Let them know that God created all of us for a reason.

Say: **God needs all of us to help one another. God also needs us to tell others about the Lord. We need to share our faith in God with other people.**

Give each child a sticker to remind them and others that they are special to God and to us.

• •

 SOMETHING SPECIAL

A Story to Share:
Who Needs Me by Florence Perry Heide

• •

GOD ERASES OUR SINS

Scripture: 1 John 1:9

PROP: A magic slate that erases

TAKE-HOME GIFT: One pencil with eraser for each child

Draw a picture on the slate. Say: **Oops! I made a mistake.** Erase the picture. Do this several times.

Show the children the pencils and ask why they have erasers.

Tell the children: **We all make mistakes. Sometimes we do things that are wrong. Sometimes we do it by accident, and sometimes we know better. That's what sin is. When we do something that we know is wrong, we sin. There are consequences to our sins. What happens if we tell lies?** (People will stop believing and trusting us.) **What happens if we are cruel to other people?** (They don't want to be around us.) Ask other similar questions, allowing the children to think of consequences to their actions.

Say: **When we do something wrong, what do we need to do?** (Apologize) **How can we show we are sorry when we have done something wrong?** (By doing our best not to do it again.)

God forgives our sins. In fact, God erases our sins. Just like I erased the mistakes I made on this slate, God erases our sins. God always lets us start all over. We need to do the best we can to be good Christians and live the way God wants us to. Sometimes we do sin (*scribble on the slate*), **but if we come to God and say, "I'm sorry," God erases that sin.** (*Erase the scribble.*)

Give each child a pencil with an eraser to take home as a reminder that God erases sin.

LET ME HELP YOU

Scripture: Matthew 25:40

TAKE-HOME GIFT: Have one index card per child. Print the Bible verse on the front of the card. On the back of each card print something the children can do to be helpful during the week. (for example, help make beds, help with dinner, clean up their room without being asked, help another child at school)

PREPARATION:

Ask several people to assist you with this beforehand. When you ask them to help you, they are to respond with comments such as, "Sorry, not today." "I'm way too busy to help you," and so forth. There will be one person who has agreed to help you. That person can reply, "Sure, I'll be glad to help."

MESSAGE:

Tell the children you need to ask some people to help you with this message. Ask the individuals you have chosen if they will help you. Of course their answers will be "No." Invite the person who agrees to help to come sit with you and the children. Look at the children and say, **I was really hoping for some help with this, and I'm glad someone finally said they would help me.**

Tell this story.

• •

LET ME HELP YOU

It was a beautiful sunny afternoon in the jungle. A little bird was running about eating berries from the bushes when she heard a horrible sound. It was the most terrifying sound she had ever heard. It sounded as though someone was in trouble. The bird looked and

> **✳ Hint ✳**
>
> Have two different colors of cards. Pink can be for 3- to 6-year-olds and green can be for 6- to 10-year-olds. Make the helping activities for each age group age appropriate. Have your helper hand out the cards for the younger children while you give cards to the older children.

looked trying to find out who was making all of that noise. Finally she came upon a huge tiger who was trapped in the thicket.

"What happened to you?" asked the bird.

"I was trying to hide from some hunters who wanted to shoot me and make me into a rug. I crawled under here hoping to be safe and I got stuck and I can't get out. The thorns are piercing my skin," replied the tiger.

"Let me help you," said the bird.

"Oh, how can a tiny bird like you help a big tiger like me?" groaned the tiger.

The little bird began to pull apart the thorns with her beak. She pulled and pulled and pulled. After a while the thicket gave way and the tiger was free. He crawled out.

"You saved my life. How can I ever thank you?" the tiger asked.

The little bird thought for a moment and replied, "You can help someone else who needs help," she said. The bird and the tiger headed off for their homes. As the tiger was nearing his den, he heard a squealing sound. There on the ground was a baby squirrel.

"What's wrong?" asked the tiger.

"I was out playing and gathering nuts and I got lost," whimpered the squirrel. "Now it's getting dark and I can't find my way back to the tree where my family lives. It's cold out here."

"I can help you find your family," said the tiger.

The tiger helped the squirrel find his family. The squirrel and her family were happy to be reunited.

"You saved my life!" said the squirrel. "Is there something I can do to help you?"

"Not really," said the tiger. "But someday you will come across someone who needs your help. Be sure to help them just as I have helped you."

"That's a good idea. I will," said the squirrel.

• •

Say: **God wants us to help each other. If we all took the time to help one another, our world would be a much happier and better place.**

Explain to your helper that this is where you will need help.

Say: **We are going to give each of you a card with the Bible verse written on it. On the back is something you can do to help another person this week. See how many people you can help. And when they thank you, be sure and tell them to show their thanks by helping someone else.**

MY BACKPACK IS HEAVY

Scripture: Psalm 38:18

PROPS: A backpack, rocks in different weights and sizes

TAKE-HOME GIFT: (Optional) Give each child a rock to remind them that sin is heavy.

Ask the children if they have ever done something wrong. They will admit it—rather sheepishly. Reassure them that you do things that are wrong also.

Ask one of the older children to help you. Have the child put on the backpack. Ask the child if the backpack is too heavy. They will say no, they can carry it easily.

Tell this story.

• •

MY BACKPACK IS HEAVY

Colin was hurriedly walking to school because he was late. He hadn't gotten up when his mother told him to, so he'd had to rush to get ready. *(Add a rock in the backpack.)* He got mad at his mom and was rude to her. *(Put a rock into the backpack.)* He hadn't finished his homework, or even started the art project he was supposed to turn in that morning.

When Colin got to school, he saw Christopher. Colin didn't like him, so he made a horrible face at him. *(Make a horrible face. Add a rock to the backpack.)*

In his classroom his teacher said, "Colin, put your art project on the counter and your homework on my desk."

"Oh, I don't have them. My dog ripped them up," Colin told her. Colin didn't even have a dog. *(Add two large rocks.)*

"You'll have to stay after school every day until you complete your homework and do your art project," said Mr. Wilson.

"Fat chance!" said Colin. *(Add two large rocks.)*

At recess, Colin was mean to Katy. She hadn't done anything to bug Colin. Colin just felt like being mean, so he was. *(Add another rock.)*

Colin's class had a math test. Since he hadn't studied, Colin copied the answers from Elizabeth. *(Add two very large rocks.)*

At lunch time Colin discovered he had forgotten his lunch, so he stole Robert's. *(Add several very large rocks.)*

"Colin, go to the principal's office this minute!" said Mr. Wilson.

As he walked to the principal's office, Colin felt scared and guilty.

"What happened Colin?" asked Mrs. Becker. "Why did Mr. Wilson send you to see me?"

"Well, I got up late and I was rude to my mom. *(Remove a rock.)* I didn't finish my homework, and I haven't even started the art project that was due today. *(Remove a rock.)* Then when I got to school, I saw that Christopher kid. I don't like him, so I made a face like this at him. *(Make the face. Remove a rock.)* When Mr. Wilson asked us to turn in our homework and art project, I lied and told him that my dog ate them. I don't even have a dog. *(Remove a rock.)* Then I was mean to Katy on the playground, just because I felt like it. *(Remove a rock.)* After recess, we had a math test, but I didn't study last night. So I copied Elizabeth's paper. She always gets A's in math. *(Remove a rock.)* Then it was time for lunch. I found out I had forgotten mine, so I took Robert's lunch. *(Remove a rock.)* That's when Mr. Wilson got really mad and sent me to see you.

"Colin, I'm glad you decided to be honest with me. I can understand how you felt when things went wrong. But it's wrong to be rude, lie, cheat, and steal," said Mrs. Becker. "It's much better to be honest about things. It's also important to be kind to other people, even people we don't like."

"I know," said Colin. "I'm really sorry, and I promise not to do any of it again."

"I forgive you, Colin," said Mrs. Becker. "But there are consequences to our behavior. You do need to be punished. You will have to stay after school every day this week. Today you will do the homework you didn't do over the weekend.

"I will ask Mr. Wilson to make up a new math test, which you can take tomorrow after school.

"On Wednesday, you can complete your art project.

"Thursday, you will write letters of apology to each of the people you hurt, including your mom, Christopher, Elizabeth, Katy, Robert, Mr. Wilson, and myself.

"On Friday, you will write down all of the things you did wrong today and better ways to handle things.

"I am going to call your parents so that we can discuss what happened today."

"I guess I deserve it," said Colin. "I'm really sorry. I promise never to do anything like that again, ever." *(Remove the rest of the rocks.)*

• •

Ask the child who was carrying the backpack:

How did it feel to carry all that sin around? (Heavy, bad, I didn't like it.)

Say: **Sin is heavy. It makes us feel bad. When we confess our sins, ask forgiveness, and promise to do better, we start to feel better. God forgives us when we sin, but God wants us to show we mean we are sorry. To show we mean that we are sorry, we have to remember not to do those things again. Remember that God loves you very much, and God always forgives you.**

Give each child a rock to take home to remind them that sin is heavy.

1. As you prepare the materials, make sure that the backpack is indeed too heavy to carry when filled with rocks.

2. If the child helping looks too burdened, remove the backpack and let him or her sit down.

3. When you do remove the backpack from the child, the others will want to show how strong they are. Let some of the children try to lift the backpack.

PUZZLE: WHAT IS THIS?

 Unscramble the following words. Print the letters in the proper spaces.

LEASTING ⓪ __ __ __ __ __ __ __

TEACHING __ __ __ __ Ⓞ __ __

BNIEG NAEM __ __ __ __ __ __ __ __ Ⓞ

NESSRUDE __ __ __ __ __ __ Ⓞ __

Print the circled letters here ____ ____ ____ ____.

How does God feel about these? What can we do to keep from doing things like this?

WE'LL SEE

Scripture: Proverbs 24:32

Say: When I was about your age, I used to ask my parents if I could do things.

"Can I go to the movies with my friends on Saturday night?"

"We'll see," would be their reply.

"Mom, we have a day off from school next week. Can you and I go shopping and out to lunch?"

"We'll see," would be my mother's reply.

"Mom, Sally asked me to spend the night at her house on Friday. Can I, please, oh please?"

"We'll see," she would say.

"Dad, could you help me work on my Scout badge this weekend?"

"We'll see," he would say.

Sometimes "We'll see" turned out to be "Yes, you may." Then there were times when it meant "No." I got so tired of hearing "We'll see."

One day I asked my parents why they always said, "We'll see." They explained that sometimes they had to talk about it and decide if what I wanted to do was a good thing for me to do. Sometimes they weren't sure what their plans were, and they wanted to make sure it worked out for me to do something. My mom said something that really made me think. She told me that she didn't want to make a promise to me and have to break it later. My parents had always taught me about the importance of keeping promises, and that it was very important not to break promises.

I thought about what she had said, and it made sense. In fact, I decided that my parents were really being considerate of me by saying, "We'll see." That way they didn't make promises and have to break them. Once in a while there was an emergency that came up that forced them to break a promise, and I understood that. But it didn't happen very often.

We'll see is an answer you can use too. Sometimes one of your friends might want you to do something that you aren't sure you want to do. Maybe you just don't want to do it or maybe it doesn't sound like it is such a good idea. You can say, "I'll see." Then you can go home and talk about it with your parents and think about it. After you have done that you can give your friend an answer.

God knows we are faced with many difficult decisions, and God wants us to think about things and make sure we are doing the right thing. I think that's why God invented the phrase, "We'll see." or "I'll see." Sometimes, after we have thought about something, we can say, "Yes, that sounds like a good thing to do." Sometimes we will have to say, "No, I can't do that."

The next time you ask your parents if you can do something and they say, "We'll see," remember they are saying that because they love you and want to decide what is best for you. They don't want to break promises to you. The next time you are faced with a decision and you aren't sure what to do say, "I'll see," and go home and talk it over with your parents and decide what is best to do.

Chapter 6: The Seasons

The messages in this section deal with the four seasons of the year. The seasons remind us that God is continually recreating our world each day.

These worship talks can become a part of the worship service on Creation found on pages 164-65.

IT'S A WINTER WONDERLAND!

Scripture: Psalm 147:16-17

PROPS: Bring in snow (if available), ice cubes and color photographs of winter.

TAKE-HOME GIFT: Give each child a snowflake with the above verse printed on it.

Say: **Winter is cold isn't it? There are no leaves on most of the trees. There are no flowers blooming. There is snow on the ground. God created winter to give the earth a rest. The earth and plants are resting so they can begin to grow again in the spring. The trees have lost their leaves. When the trees are without leaves, they don't need as much water. That allows them to get ready to make new leaves in the spring.**

Just like we sleep at night so we can be strong the next day, the earth has to sleep during the winter so it can be strong in the spring. The earth needs to be strong so it can give us the things we need. What kinds of things do we get from the earth? (Food, wood for houses, pencils, furniture, and so forth)

Show the children the snow and pictures of snow. Say: **Did you know that every snowflake that falls from the sky is different? There are no two snowflakes that are alike. Who creates the snowflakes?** (God) **Isn't it awesome that God creates all of those different snowflakes? Just like each of us is different, so are things in nature. What are some of the things we can do in winter that we can't do other times of the year?** (Skiing, ice skating outdoors, sledding, building snow people, and so forth) **God created winter so the earth can rest, but also so we can have different activities to enjoy.**

Have the children create snowflakes out of white paper. Let each child print something they like best about winter on their snowflakes. If desired, children can glue white glitter on their snowflakes. Display them on a bulletin board or wall.

 SOMETHING SPECIAL

A Story to Share
The Friendly Snowflake by M. Scott Peck
  Tell this story to the children.

IT'S SPRING

Scripture: Revelation 21:5

PROPS: Spring things, (seeds, flowering bulbs, blooming branches) and color photographs of spring.

TAKE-HOME GIFT: Give each child a packet of flower seeds with the Bible verse attached.

Say: **Do you notice any changes going on around you?** (Trees are budding, flowers blooming, days getting longer and warmer, and so forth) **Why do you think this is happening?** (It's spring.) **Who created spring?** (God) **Why?** (Let them share their thoughts.)

Explain: **Spring is a rebirth of nature. Remember in the fall when the leaves died and fell off the trees? During the winter there were no leaves on the trees. There were no flowers outside. The grass died and was brown. Remember how the earth was covered in snow, frost, and ice. God was letting the earth rest during the winter so that in spring the trees could grow new leaves and the flowers could grow again. Spring is here. Look at all of the changes around us. This is God's miracle of creation.**

God is making new leaves for the trees and new blossoms for the flowers. Every year we can count on God to replenish the earth with new beauty.

 SOMETHING SPECIAL

A Story to Share
Spring Is a New Beginning
by Joan Walsh Anglund
Make this into story cards. See page 166 for instructions.

 **Idea**

Give each child a piece of white construction paper and a green crayon. Have them draw a flower stem and leaves on their papers. Paint their hands with a variety of colors (pink, purple, yellow, orange, red). Let them make handprint flowers. Staple these to your bulletin board to make a flower garden.

SUMMER FUN

Scripture: Genesis 8:22

PROPS: Summer things (flowers, leaves from trees), color photographs of summer

Ask: **How do you know it's summer?** (It is hot outside, the days are longer, no school, and so forth) **Why do you think God made summer?** (So we can grow food to eat.) **Summer is a time of growing. The trees grow bigger, flowers grow and food grows. We need summer to make food grow, so we can harvest it in the fall and eat it during winter and spring. What kinds of foods grow during the summer?** (Fruits, vegetables, and so forth) **What else is nice about summer?** (We can play outside more, we can have picnics, and so forth) Show the children pictures of summer time and let them tell you about them.

Ask the children what season will come after summer. (Autumn, fall). Talk about winter and spring and summer. **Every year the seasons come, each season lasting the same amount of time, each season bringing something special with it. Every day, every season, every year God continues the miracle of creation.**

SOMETHING SPECIAL

A Story to Share
The Summer Night by Charlotte Zolotow
Read this to the children.

 Idea

Have the children create a summer story. They can create this as a group or individually. Let them illustrate the stories.

AWESOME AUTUMN

Scripture: Daniel 2:21

PROPS: Autumn leaves in a variety of colors, acorns, color photographs of autumn foods (for example, pumpkins). Glue some white glitter to a couple of leaves to make them look like they have frost on them.

Ask the children if they notice any changes outside. **What is happening? Why do you think these things are happening? Who is making them happen?**

I took a walk the other day. It was beautiful outside. The sky was bright blue and the sun was shining, but there was a chill in the air.

I noticed that the leaves on the trees weren't green any longer. They were turning different shades of red, orange and yellow. (Show them the leaves.) **Some of the leaves had fallen to the ground and turned brown.** (Show them brown leaves.) **There were acorns from the oak trees on the ground.** (Show them the acorns.)

What do you think will happen to these things? (The leaves will fertilize the soil and the acorns will grow into new trees.)

These leaves and acorns allow God's miracle of creation to happen. It's getting colder out now. The days are getting shorter. One morning I even noticed frost on everything. (Show them the leaves with frost.)

I've seen pumpkins too. What do we do with pumpkins? (Carve them into Jack-o-lanterns, make them into bread and pie.

Idea

Make an "Awesome Autumn" book. Give each child a sheet of white construction paper with the words "Autumn Is" printed across the top. Let the children draw autumn pictures and finish the sentence. Have the children sign their drawings. Ask two children to create a front and back cover. Staple the pages together to make a book to add to your resource center or church library.

Show pictures). **God created pumpkins so we could do these things with them.**

What do we call this season? (Fall, Autumn) **Autumn lets the world get ready for winter. If it got cold too fast, it would be too hard on the earth. Autumn allows the trees to lose their leaves; it allows the earth to cool down gradually so it can get ready for winter.**

We harvest crops during autumn. These crops were planted in the spring and grew all summer. Now they are ready to be harvested so we will have food to eat. Autumn is filled with God's miracles. God has helped the food grow so it is ready to be harvested and eaten.

Ask the children if they remember how winter helps the earth. Ask them to tell you what happens in the spring and the summer. Help them understand the seasons are necessary for the earth and for us. Explain that God created the earth for our needs and enjoyment. This is one of the ways God shows love for us.

🎁 SOMETHING SPECIAL

A Story to Share
Say It! by Charlotte Zolotow
Read this story to the children.

ART: GOD'S BEAUTIFUL WORLD

Draw and color a picture of the season we are enjoying now.

Chapter 7: Celebration Days

The church year is filled with days of celebrations.

These days allow us to celebrate our faith in God. They

call us to reflect upon our faith and to share it with others.

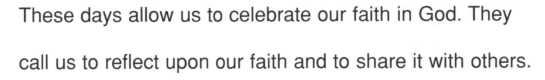

Celebrate God's special days with your children. Be

filled with the joy and the enthusiasm of a child.

BIBLE PRESENTATION DAY: WHAT A GREAT BOOK!

Scripture: 1 Peter 1:25

PROPS: 1 copy of the Bible the children will receive, 1 book of religious songs, biography of a famous biblical person, book of rules, Bible storybook (individual story book), fiction book (Place these items in a paper bag that is hidden from view.)

TAKE-HOME GIFT: 1 Bible per child who is due to receive a Bible, 1 scripture card per child for the other children

Tell the children you forgot something. Retrieve your bag of books.

Show them the books you have. **I like to read about famous people, so I found this book about Ruth. She was a fascinating woman in the Old Testament. I like to sing songs, so I found this book of songs. Look at all of the wonderful songs there are in it. I needed rules for playing a game on my computer. Do you know what? I found one. I like to read stories, so I found a good story to read. I know I will enjoy my books.**

There is one more book I want to show you. It's my Bible. It's the best book I have. It is a marvelous book. It has stories about famous people. See here is the story about Ruth. It has songs to sing. (Show them Psalms.) **We sing many songs based on the Psalms. It has rules for how we should live. See here are the Ten Commandments. Following**

those is important, so I need to know where they are. The Bible has lots of good stories to read. When I am worried, frightened, or sad, there are passages in the Bible I can read that remind me that God loves me and stays right with me no matter what happens. That makes me feel better.

Several people will receive Bibles today. This Bible is our gift to you.

☀ Ideas ☀

1. Give each child a children's Bible with colorful illustrations, charts and commentaries.
2. Put a bookplate in the front that tells the Bible is a gift from your church. Inscribe each child's name on the bookplate.
3. Ask the parents of the children receiving Bibles to be present for the Presentation Ceremony.
4. After each child receives a Bible, turn to a passage and read it together.

PUZZLE: GETTING TO KNOW YOUR BIBLE

Use your Bible to complete these answers.

1. ___ ___ ___ those who wait for the LORD shall renew their strength, they shall mount up with wings like eagles, they shall run and not be weary, they shall walk and not faint. (Isaiah 40:31)

2. ___ ___ ___ LORD is my shepherd, I shall not want. (Psalm 23:1)

3. Every ___ ___ ___ ___ of God proves true; he is a shield to those who take refuge in him. (Proverbs 30:5)

4. And she gave birth to her firstborn son and wrapped him in bands ___ ___ cloth, and laid him in a manger, because there was no place for them in the inn. (Luke 2:7)

5. Blessed are ___ ___ ___ pure in heart, for they will see God. (Matthew 5:8)

6. My help comes from the ___ ___ ___ ___, who made heaven and earth. (Psalm 121:2)

7. O give thanks to the LORD. . . for his steadfast love ___ ___ ___ ___ ___ ___ ___ forever. (Psalm 136:1)

8. For the LORD is good; his steadfast love endures ___ ___ ___ ___ ___ ___ ___, and his faithfulness to all generations. (Psalm 100:5)

Print each word you found in the spaces below. They spell out another Bible verse.

___ ___ ___   ___ ___ ___ ___   ___ ___ ___ ___ ___ ___ ___   ___ ___ ___   ___ ___ ___ ___ ___

___ ___ ___ ___ ___ ___ ___   ___ ___ ___ ___ ___ ___ ___ ___ ___.

(1 ___E___ER 1:___ ___)

When you finish this puzzle, give it to your Sunday school teacher who will give you a special prize.

HOLY COMMUNION: A MEAL WITH JESUS

Scripture: Matthew 26:17-29; Mark 14:17-25; Luke 22:14-20

PROPS: Bread and juice (wine)

Ask the children why we eat and drink. Their response of satisfying our hunger and thirst will naturally lead you into a discussion of our need for Communion. We are hungry to be nourished by God's love and forgiveness. We need to quench our thirst to stay alive in God's love. Explain that Jesus "invites" all of us to share this meal with him.

Tell the story of the Last Supper. Explain that God realizes we will make mistakes and wants to help us. Talk about the importance of both saying and showing we are sorry. Remind them that Communion is God's way of saying, "I forgive you, and I love you."

Explain that during Bible times, the people ate these kinds of foods for some of their meals. Children already know we need to eat good food for our nourishment, health, and growth. Communion is what we need to nourish our soul so we have strength to do God's work. Ask the children how we can share the gift of God's love with others? **What can we do to help others?**

Explain that when Jesus lived, the bread was hard and difficult to eat. To make it easier to eat, the people dipped their pieces of bread into the wine (juice).

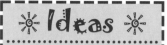

1. See the calls to worship on page 21, and benedictions on page 96.

2. Use this Worship Talk as part of the Communion Service.

 SOMETHING SPECIAL

A Song to Sing
"We Come to Your Table" by Carey Landry in *Hi God*, 2

Invite the children to sing this during worship on Communion Sunday.

Since this song is about bringing gifts, talk with the children about the gift God gave us on Christmas Eve. Let that lead into a discussion about the gift Jesus gave to us on Good Friday. Explain that because Jesus gave his life, we must come to his table offering our gifts. We can bring gifts of love and thanksgiving when we come to Communion. With this song, we are offering our gift of music.

ASH WEDNESDAY: SAY YOUR PRAYERS

Scripture: 1 Thessalonians 5:17

PROPS: A piece of play dough (see recipe page 159), a large bag of small pretzels, baskets for pretzels

TAKE-HOME GIFT: One pretzel per child.

Explain: **Ash Wednesday is the beginning of the time we call Lent. Lent is the forty days preceding Easter. It is a time for us to reflect upon our lives and to think about improving them. It is a time to learn more about Jesus.**

During Lent we can spend extra time praying and talking to God. Sometimes we forget to say prayers, and that makes God feel very sad. God likes it when we pray.

A long time ago there were some children, just like you, who sometimes forgot to say their prayers. There was a monk who felt very bad about this, and he thought of a way to help children remember to say their prayers.

(Take out the dough and make it into a pretzel shape. Don't say anything. Let the children watch what you do.)

Do you know what this looks like? (A pretzel) **Yes, it looks like a pretzel. The monk made a shape that looked like a child in prayer. The child's head is bowed and the child's hands are folded. He baked it in the oven and it became a pretzel.**

Pretzels can remind us to say our prayers.

When it is time to dispense the ashes, explain that the ashes remind us of our sins. They are reminders for us to ask God to forgive our sins.

☀ Ideas ☀

1. Say a prayer with the children and let them eat a pretzel.
2. Give each child a plastic food storage bag with seven pretzels and a prayer inside. Tell them to take it home and say this prayer every day. After they finish the prayer, they can eat one pretzel.
3. See pages 62-89 for prayer activities.
4. Combine with the puzzles found on pages 65-66
5. Fill several baskets with pretzels. Let the children distribute these to the congregation. Say a prayer and eat the pretzels.

PALM SUNDAY: IT'S A PARADE

Scriptures: Matthew 21:1-11; Mark 11:1-11; Luke 19:28-44

PROPS: Palm branches

Tell the story of Palm Sunday. Explain that the people had a parade for Jesus. Ask the children to share their parade experiences. Have they ever participated in a parade? How? Have they ever watched a parade? What was it like?

Explain that the word *HOSANNA* was used to show great excitement, praise, and love for Jesus. It can also mean "save now."

Tell them that we are entering into what we call "Holy Week" and we will be remembering the Last Supper on Maundy Thursday and the Crucifixion on Good Friday. We must experience all of these things, even though they are very sad, before we can celebrate the joy of the Resurrection on Easter.

☀ Ideas ☀

1. Use with the calls to worship on page 22, and benedictions on page 98.
2. Let the children have their own Palm Sunday parade. They can march, sing songs, and play rhythm instruments. Have them wave palm branches and shout "Hosanna! Blessed is the one who comes in the name of the Lord!" Try parading around your meeting room, outdoors, and around the block.
3. Have the children parade into the sanctuary and carry palms. Let the children distribute the palms to the congregation.

GOOD FRIDAY: CRUCIFY HIM!

Scriptures: Matthew 27:15-44; Mark 15:1-47; Luke 23; John 18:28–19:42

PROPS: A large cross (if possible, the size they used to crucify Jesus). Put two smaller crosses on each side of it. Place a hammer and nails nearby, and a whip similar to the one they used on Jesus.

Share the story of what happened on Good Friday. Let the children examine closely and touch the cross, hammer, nails, and whip.

Ask them to share their thoughts about Good Friday and what happened on that day.

· ·

 SOMETHING SPECIAL

A Story to Share
Tale of Three Trees by Angel Elwell Hunt

Use the book to read the story, allowing the children to see the lovely illustrations. The story needs no discussion. Simply dismiss them with the words, **Thank you for listening.**

· ·

```
☀ Idea ☀
· · · · · · · · · · · · · · · · · · · · · · · · · ·

Make three large crosses out of wood. Insert them into the ground in front of
your building. Drape the center cross in black. Take the children on a "Walk to
Calvary." Ask other adults to help you reenact the Crucifixion story for the chil-
dren. Have a group of people shout, "Crucify Him! Crucify Him!"
```

EASTER: JESUS LIVES!

Scriptures: Matthew 28; Mark 16; Luke 24:1-49; John 20:1-18

PROPS: A large rock

Reenact the Easter story. Use the large rock as the entrance to the tomb. Ask several women to dress like Mary and the other women who went to the tomb. Ask other children to portray the angel sitting on the rock, and Jesus.

After the children are seated by "the tomb," Mary and the other women can enter talking about anointing Jesus' body. When they arrive at the tomb, let them share their surprise at not finding Jesus there. Have the angel speak to them. The women can turn to see all of the children. Let them sit down and talk about what has happened.

Encourage a conversation about what has happened between the women and the children.

While the women are talking to the children, have Jesus enter and join them. Let Jesus talk to the women and children.

SOMETHING SPECIAL

A Story to Share

"Even Unto the End of the World" by Eleanor M. Jewitt from *It's Time for Easter,* compiled by Elizabeth Sechrist

Tell this story to the children. Let it stand on its own. When you are finished thank the children and let them leave.

Some songs to sing

"New Hope" and "Oh, Yes Lord Jesus Lives" by Carey Landry from *Hi God, 2* by Carey Landry

Invite the children or your children's choir to sing one of these songs during the Easter worship service. This can be the children's Easter offering.

☀ Ideas ☀

1. Easter calls to worship are found on pages 23-24.

2. Benedictions for Easter are on page 100.

3. Easter prayers are found on pages 74-75.

4. Take another "Walk to Calvary" (See Good Friday ideas on page 130.) This time the cross is draped in white.

MOTHER'S OR FATHER'S DAY: HAPPY MOTHER'S/FATHERS' DAY

Scripture: Exodus 20:12

PROPS:

Photos of mothers/fathers with their children. Include individual posed pictures of each mother with her children and each father with his children. Also take candid photos of children and parents. Mount them on paper and have them available for viewing.

☀ Hint ☀

Be sensitive to different family structures

Make an art gallery that says "Our Mothers/Fathers with Their Children."

Show the children the pictures you have taken of them with their mothers/fathers. Ask: **What kinds of things do you see happening in these pictures?**

 VARIATION

Ask the children to come forward and to bring their mothers and/or fathers with them. Include grandmothers and grandfathers if you wish. Ask the mothers and fathers to share their thoughts and feelings about what it is like to be a parent. **What is the best part of being a mom or dad? What is the hardest part of being a mom or dad? Ask the children to share their thoughts on what it is like to be a son or daughter. What do you like best about your mother or father?** Let grandparents share their thoughts on being parents and grandparents.

☀ Ideas ☀

1. Prayers for Mother's and Father's Day are on pages 75-76.
2. See the puzzles on pages 132-33.

PUZZLE:
WHO IS SPECIAL?

Color: M: Red   O: Green

PUZZLE: WHO'S SPECIAL?

 Color: D: Orange A: Red

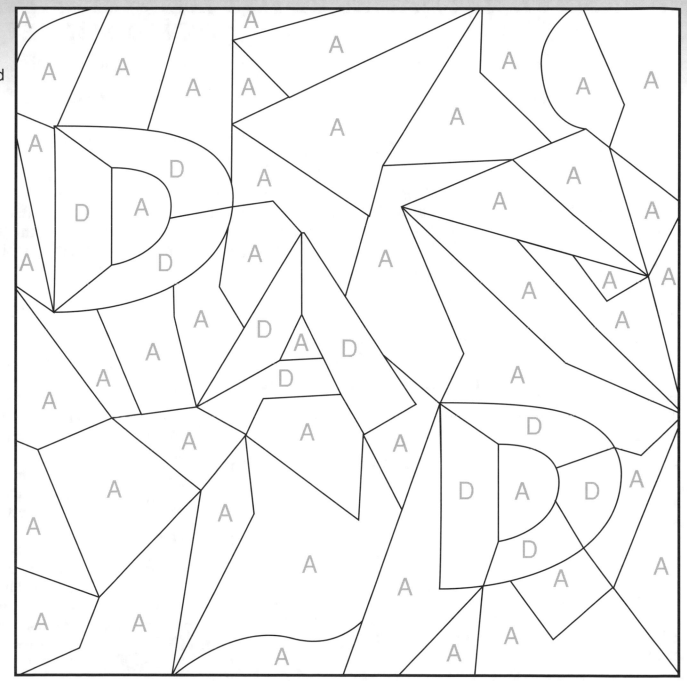

THANKSGIVING: THANKS BE TO GOD

Scripture: Psalm 100:4; John 21:15-17

PROPS: Borrow a grocery cart from a grocery store.

Prior to this talk provide a grocery bag with the words "Feed My Sheep" written on the outside. Let each person take one home to fill with non-perishable foods. The children can place their bags in the grocery cart in a designated area. Donate food to the local food pantry.

Tell the children the story of Thanksgiving. Let them know that God wants us to share what we have with others. We can show our thanks to God for all we have by sharing with others. Ask the children to share their thoughts on Thanksgiving and sharing.

> ✳ **Ideas** ✳
>
> 1. Thanksgiving calls to worship are on pages 25-26.
> 2. A Thanksgiving litany is on pages 49-50.
> 3. Thanksgiving Prayers and Responses are on pages 76-78.
> 4. Thanksgiving activities are on pages 26 and 27.
> 6. Use this talk with the "Give Thanks and Share" worship service on page 158.

SOMETHING SPECIAL

A Song to Sing
"It's a Miracle" by William J. Gaither in *Sing 'n' Celebrate for Kids*, vol. 2

Invite the children or children's choir to sing this for a Thanksgiving worship service.

Talk about miracles. Ask the children to tell about miracles they have seen. Explain that our creation, our being here, is a miracle. We are all miracles.

THE FIRST SUNDAY IN ADVENT: DON'T FORGET JESUS

Scripture: Isaiah 7:14

PROP: An Advent wreath

On the first Sunday in Advent explain that the word *advent* means the arrival of something. Ask who is going to arrive? (Jesus) Explain that Advent is a time we use to get ready for the birth of Jesus.

Ask:: **What are some of the things you do at home to get ready for Christmas?** (Decorate, bake, make/buy presents, send cards, and so forth)

If you look around you will see that we already have something different. What is it? (Advent wreath) **What colors are the candles**? (3 purple/blue, 1 pink and 1 white). Explain: **The purple (blue) candles tell us that a King will be born on Christmas. Who is that King?** (Jesus). **The pink candle reminds us that Jesus is a person just like the rest of us. The white candle symbolizes the purity of Christ.**

Today we will light the first purple (blue) candle. This is the candle of promise. God promised to send Jesus to us. Jesus promised to save us from our sins. Why do you think God sent Jesus to us? (Let the children share their ideas.)

> ✳ **Ideas** ✳
>
> 1. Use an Advent call to worship from pages 28-30.
> 2. Try an Advent benediction found on pages 102.
> 3. See pages 159-61 for an Advent worship service.

Explain: **God was very disappointed that people on earth were not following the Lord's rules. God knew that people needed a person to come and teach them about the Lord. God sent Jesus to do that. Jesus would come as a baby, be a child, and learn the things children learn. He would grow into a man who would teach people about God and how to live according to God's will.**

 SOMETHING SPECIAL

A Story to Share
"The City That Forgot About Christmas" by Mary Warren in *Christmas Classics for Children*

Ask the children if they have ever forgotten about Christmas. (NO!) **Why not? Do you think you could forget about Christmas?** (NO!) Ask children why we celebrate Christmas? (It is when Jesus was born.) **Yes, we put up decorations, send and receive cards, get a vacation from school, and get presents, but the most important thing to remember is that we are celebrating the birth of Jesus.**

Let me share a story with you. It's about some people who forgot about Christmas. Read or tell the story. Dismiss them with a gentle reminder to remember why we celebrate this day.

SECOND SUNDAY IN ADVENT: COMING IN HOPE

Scripture: Psalm 130:7

PROPS: Put up the manger scene. Include a variety of barn animals and an empty manger. (Mary, Joseph, Jesus, the angels, and shepherds are added on Christmas Eve.)

On the second Sunday in Advent, talk about how we continue to prepare for Christmas and the birth of Christ. Ask the children if they notice anything different. (They will point out the manger scene.) Ask them what is missing (Mary, Joseph, Jesus, angels, shepherds).

Explain that we are waiting for Jesus with hope in our hearts. We are waiting for Mary and Joseph to arrive. We are waiting for Jesus' birthday (Jesus to be born).

Today we are going to light the second candle on the Advent wreath. That is the candle of hope. Why do you think we call it the candle of hope? (Let the children share their thoughts.) **When Christ came, he brought hope into the world. We hope that the world will become a better place to live because of his birth.**

Light the first and second candles on the Advent wreath.

 SOMETHING SPECIAL

A Story to Share
All Those Mothers at the Manger by Norma Farber
Read this to the children.
A Song to Sing
"Come Lord Jesus" by Carey Landry in *Hi God, 2*
Talk about God's invitation to open our hearts to Jesus and his everlasting love. Invite the children or your children's choir to sing this for worship.

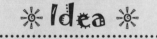
☀ **Idea** ☀

Use the appropriate verses for Advent calls to worship, pages 28-30, and benedictions, page 102.

THIRD SUNDAY IN ADVENT: CHRISTMAS PEACE

Scripture: John 14:27

PROPS: Prior to the service, add undecorated Christmas trees to the sanctuary decorations.

On the third Sunday in Advent, ask the children to look around to see what has been added this week (Christmas trees). Ask: **Why do we have Christmas trees?** (To decorate). Explain that the Christmas tree is an evergreen. It always stays green. It reminds us of the everlasting love of Christ. It reminds us of everlasting life. If we accept Christ as our Lord and Savior, we will have everlasting life and go to heaven to live with God after our life on earth is finished.

Tell the children you will light the third candle on the Advent wreath. This is the candle of peace. Jesus came into the world to bring peace. God doesn't want us to be at war with others. God doesn't want us to fight and harm each other. God wants us to live in peace. Jesus came to teach us about living in peace.

Light the first, second, and third candles on the Advent wreath.

> ☀ **Idea** ☀
>
> Use the appropriate lines/verses from Advent calls to worship on pages 28–30 and Advent Benedictions (page 102).

 SOMETHING SPECIAL

A Story to Share
"Little Tree and His Wish" by Viola Rutz in *Christmas Classics for Children*

Have the trees and the manger on the altar when you share this story.

A Song to Sing
"What Can We Give to the King?" by Barry McGuire and Mike Deasy from *The Birthday Party*

Talk about the different ways we have of showing love for one another, for our families, and for God. Love is the best gift we can give.

FOURTH SUNDAY IN ADVENT: COMING IN JOY

Scripture: Isaiah 55:12

PROPS: Prior to the service, place some poinsettias on the altar.

Ask the children to tell you what has been added this week (poinsettias). Ask why we have poinsettias at Christmas. (Because they are pretty.) Explain that there are many legends about the things that took place when Jesus was born. There is a legend about the poinsettia that says a young girl picked some plants to take to Mary. When she gave the plants to Mary, they burst into the beautiful flowering plants we see now. The red blooms that

> ☀ **Idea** ☀
>
> Use the appropriate verses for Advent calls to worship (pages 28-30) and Advent benedictions (page 102).

look like a flower are actually leaves. The flower is the tiny yellow part in the center of the red leaves. The red reminds us of the blood that will be shed by Christ on Good Friday. If you also have white poinsettias, explain that reminds us of the purity of Christ.

Tell the children you will light the fourth candle on the Advent wreath. It is the candle of JOY. **Why do you think we call it the candle of JOY?** (We are happy Jesus is born. Jesus brought joy into the world.)

Explain that new babies bring us joy and happiness. Explain that the candle we are lighting today is a different color than the others. **What color is it?** (Pink). Explain that pink reminds us that Jesus was a real person. It represents the flesh of Jesus.

Light all four candles on the Advent wreath.

 SOMETHING SPECIAL

A Story to Share
"The Mysterious Star" by Joanne Marxhausen in *Christmas Classics for Children*
Let this story stand on its own. It needs no discussion.

A Song to Sing
"When God Becomes a Baby" by Joanne Barrett/Ron E. Long from *Hark, the Herald Angel*
Explain to the children that Jesus was a child just like they are. He had to do many of the same things we do.

CHRISTMAS EVE: IT'S A BABY BOY!

Scriptures: Matthew 1:18-25 and Luke 2:1-20

PROPS:

Have the baby Jesus in a manger. If possible have a real baby in your manger. Ask the baby's parents to portray Mary and Joseph. Have them dress appropriately and act the parts. Hang a shining star from the ceiling so that it is over the manger.

Ask the children to tell you what they see. Let Mary and Joseph share their feelings about their new child, and introduce the baby to the children and tell them about his or her birth and what it means.

Choose four children to light the candles on the Advent wreath. Each child can light one candle. As they light the candles, have them say, "This is the candle of promise. This is the candle of hope. This is the candle of peace. this is the candle of joy."

Ask Mary and Joseph to light the Christ candle. "This is the candle of love."

☀ Ideas ☀

1. Choose a spoken and musical call to worship for Christmas Eve (pages 30-32) and a Christmas Eve benediction (page 104).

2. Try a Christmas prayer and prayer response (pages 78-79).

SOMETHING SPECIAL

A Story to Share
The Littlest Angel by Charles Tazewell

PROPS: Battered up box with the following inside: silk flower, colored rocks, worn dog collar, butterfly magnet, blue egg shell, Christmas star (nonblinking variety), long extension cord

Plug in the extension cord and have it next to where you will be seated to tell the story. Hide the box and the star so they are not visible.

As you tell the story, when the Littlest Angel receives his beloved box, reach for the box and set it unopened on your lap. When the story reveals the contents of the box, open it, and one by one take out each object and show it to the children without interrupting the telling of the story. Simply hold the object up for them to see and put it back into the box. Close the box. When the time comes for the box to rise up to heaven, plug the star into the cord and hold it high over your head.

[Beforehand, ask a volunteer to dim the lights down to almost total darkness when it is time for the star to shine.]

This story needs no discussion. This is an enthralling experience for the children.

SOMETHING SPECIAL

A Song to Sing
"The Friendly Beasts" arranged by Charles Black

Ask your children's choir to sing it. Talk about the animals that were in the stable when Jesus was born. Each animal gave a gift to Jesus.

CHRISTMAS: HAPPY BIRTHDAY, JESUS!

Scripture: Luke 2:1-20

PREPARATION/PROPS:

Have the children create gifts that they would like to give to Jesus. They can draw pictures of these gifts, or write poems or stories to give to Jesus.

Make and decorate a large sheet cake. Write "Happy Birthday, Jesus" on the cake. Put in candles. You may have a manger scene with a shining star.

Give each child the gift they made. Have the children place their gifts around the manger. Ask the children to sit before you. Look at the gifts, and let the children tell about their gifts.

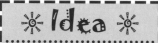

Ask each child to bring a baby gift. Donate these to an organization that serves unwed mothers or needy families.

Explain that Jesus is their Christmas gift from God. God gave Jesus to each of us as a gift. Ask the children to tell you why Jesus came to earth. (To teach us how to live and to save us from our sins.) Tell the children that they can share this gift with others. Ask them to think of ways they can do this. (Helping others, being kind, and so forth) Light the candles on the cake. Invite everyone to sing "Happy Birthday, Jesus." Ask everyone to close their eyes and say a prayer (make a wish) for Jesus. Blow out the candles, and enjoy eating the cake.

EPIPHANY: WHO'S COMING?

Scripture: Matthew 2:1-12

PROPS: A nativity scene.

Dramatize the story with Mary, Joseph, Jesus and the three Wise Men.

Tell the story of the Three Wise Men. Say: **The first said, "I bring the gift of gold, a gift fit for a King." The second said, "I bring the gift of frankincense which is a gift for a God." The third said, "I bring the gift of myrrh which is used to preserve the body for burial."**

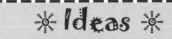

※ Ideas ※

1. Try an Epiphany call to worship found on pages 32-33
2. Try a benediction for Epiphany from page 106.
3. See the puzzles on pages 34, 35, and 107.

Explain that these were very special gifts. They were gifts that help us remember the birth, life, death, and resurrection of Jesus. The wise men can place their gifts on the altar.

 SOMETHING SPECIAL

Some Stories to Share
The Christmas Star by Marcus Pfister

Read this story to the children, allowing them to see the lovely illustrations. No discussion is needed.

The Legend of Old Befana by Tomie de Paola

Read this story to the children and allow them to see the illustrations. Remind the children that we do not have to search for Jesus the way Old Befana did. Jesus is right here with us all the time. All we have to do is ask Jesus to help us.

Chapter 8: Beginnings and Endings

Children's lives are filled with beginnings and endings. These worship talks can help them to express their feelings and concerns about these events.

COME BE BAPTIZED!

Scripture: Matthew 28:19

PROPS: The baby being baptized

Say: **Look at how beautifully made this baby is. He/She has tiny hands with teeny fingernails and little feet. See his/her eyes, ears, and mouth. (Baby's name) has everything he/she needs. God created this baby so his/her parents could share the love they have for one another with him/her. (Baby's name) is a very special gift from God. (See variation.)**

Today when (Baby's name) is baptized, the minister will use water to bless him/her in the name of the Creator (Father), Christ (Son), and Living Spirit (Holy Spirit). This is how the church promises to take care of children. His/Her parents will also make some promises.

It is important for them to keep these promises, because they are making them to God and to (Baby's name). It will be important for (Baby's name)'s parents to teach him/her about God at home and to set a good example of how Christians live. They will have to spend a lot of time teaching (Baby's name) the difference between right and wrong. When (Baby's name) is old enough, he/she can learn about God and Jesus at Sunday school and church.

You can help too. You can greet (Baby's name) when you see her/him. You can talk to her/him. It takes a baby's family and the church to help children learn about being a Christian.

 VARIATION

Hold the baby on your lap.

Add the following section before talking about baptism.

But she/he looks hungry. (Baby's name), why don't you get down off my lap and walk into the kitchen and ask the people there to give you a peanut butter and jelly sandwich.

What's wrong? Why shouldn't (Baby's name) walk into the kitchen and ask for a peanut butter and jelly sandwich? (Because he/she is too little to walk and talk.)

But he/she has feet and a mouth. (But she/he isn't big enough to use them that way yet.)

You are absolutely right. (Baby's name) is too little to do those things. That is why (Baby's name)'s parents take care of him/her.

Let the children remain up front for the baptism.

※ Hint ※

You might want to have another adult sit with the children and help them be attentive.

※ Ideas ※

1. Combine with the benedictions on page 94.
2. Use with puzzle on pages 95 and 142.

 SOMETHING SPECIAL

Some Songs to Sing
"I Am a Promise" by Bill and Gloria Gaither
"Kids Under Construction" by Bill and Gloria Gaither
in *Sing 'n' Celebrate for Kids*, vol. 2

The children can sing one of these songs when a baby is baptized during worship service.

PUZZLE: COME BE BAPTIZED

 Complete this crossword puzzle about baptism.

DOWN

1. Jesus was baptized in the _____ River. (Mark 1:9)

2. Baptism is a sign of _____ love for us.

3. We can baptize people when they are babies, children,

   or _____.

4. When Jesus was baptized, the Holy Spirit descended

   upon him in the form of a dove. God said, "You are my

   Son, the Beloved, with you I am _____ pleased."

   (Luke 3:22)

ACROSS

1. John the Baptist baptized _____. (Matthew 3:13)

2. It is important for parents to _____ their chil-

   dren about God and Jesus.

3. When we baptize people we welcome them to God's

   _____.

Print the circled letters here. _____

Unscramble them to form

this word. ___ ___ ___ ___ ___

What is important about this word?

CREATION

Scripture: Genesis 1:1–2:3

PROPS: Rocks; leaves and tree bark; flowers; pictures of the sky, ocean, mountains, animals, grass and soil, star, sun, moon

Show all of the items to the children and ask them what they have in common. **Where did they come from? How did they get there? Who created them?**

Tell the story of creation to the children. Invite comments about the world God has created for us. Ask: **Do you think any-one of us could do something like that? Why? Why not?**

Explain that God is still creating our world. Say: **When trees grow new leaves in the springtime, when flowers bloom, when it rains and snows—all of these are examples of creation.**

Talk about babies and how they are perfect examples of creation. Say: **God continues to recreate the world each and every day, each and every minute, each and every second. God never stops creating our world.**

> ✳ **Idea** ✳
>
> This worship talk can be used with the worship service "God's Creation" on pages 164–65.

 SOMETHING SPECIAL

Some Stories to Share
The Dreamer by Cynthia Rylant
And God Created Squash by Martha Whitmore Hickman
Old Turtle by Douglas Wood

Share one of these books after the above discussion, allowing the children to see the lovely illustrations.

DEATH BRINGS NEW LIFE

Scripture: John 3:16

PROPS: Dead leaves, lima beans, plant

Show the dead leaves, and ask what they are and why they died. Show the seeds and ask what they are. Ask: **Are they alive?** Let the children explain why or why not. Show the plant and ask if it is dead or alive. Ask: **How do you know? Where did the plant come from? How do plants grow? What do they need to grow?**

Explain that everything that is living will someday die. **Each year the tree gets new leaves. They bloom during the spring and grow during the summer. In the fall the leaves turn colors and fall off the trees and die. The next spring new leaves come out. This seed doesn't look alive, but there is life inside of it. If we plant it, water it, and care for it, it will grow into a living plant. Plants make new seeds so that new plants can grow.** (Break or cut open a lima bean to see how it looks inside.)

Explain that every person will die. Say: **When someone we love dies, we are sometimes very sad because we miss her/him. We can remember this person (use name) through the good things they did and the fun times we shared. Remember that when people die, they go to heaven to live with God and Jesus.**

If the person who has died had been sick or badly injured, reassure the children

> 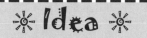 **Idea** ✳
>
> Write the children's comments on a piece of paper. Present the list to the family of the person who has died. If the person who died was a child in your children's program, make a second list and post it where the children can see it along with a picture of that child. You can also have the children draw pictures and write their thoughts about this child. Make a cover, stapling it together to make a book. Give it to the child's family.

> ✳ **Hint** ✳
>
> Adapt this worship talk to the specific situation. Use an appropriate explanation depending on the person who died.

that when people go to heaven, they will never be sick or hurt again. Say: **Sometimes the doctors cannot make someone well or fix their injuries. But when they go to heaven, God makes them better. They will never be sick or hurt again.**

 SOMETHING SPECIAL

A Song to Sing
"New Hope" by Carey Landry in *Hi God, 2*

If the person who has died has been important to the children, consider having the children sing this as a memorial.

HAPPY NEW SCHOOL YEAR!

Scripture: Luke 2:40

PROPS: A variety of school supplies

TAKE-HOME GIFT: One scripture eraser per child

Show the children the school supplies. Ask them what we use these for. Invite the children to tell how it feels to be starting a new school year. Ask: **Who is going to school for the very first time? Who is starting in a new school? Who is going to be a "new kid" at school? Who is returning to the same school, but starting a new grade?**

Explain that we often feel excited and scared about starting the new school year. Say: **Some of you are probably looking for-**ward to the new year, some of you might be scared, and maybe some of you just don't want school to start at all.**

Let the children share their thoughts and feelings. **Parents understand your feelings because they have all been through the start of a new school year or new job. Teachers understand too because they know children may feel this way. God understands too.**

Sometimes when we are scared, we'd kind of like to have our moms and dads stay with us, but moms and dads can't stay at school with us. God stays with us and helps us wherever we go. Remember that God will stay with you at school all the time. God will be with you when you don't understand something, when you learn new things, and even when you take a test.

☀ **Ideas** ☀

1. Use the "Prayer for the New School Year" on pages 68-69.
2. Combine with the puzzle on page 145.

PUZZLE: BACK TO SCHOOL

Draw lines through each clue. Clues go down or across. Two clues go in two directions. They are _____ and _____. Which two clues are listed twice? _____ and _____. When you are finished, you will have several letters left over. Circle them with red pencil. What do they spell? _____

```
L  R  E  C  E  S  S  F  I  E  L  D  T
U  M  U  S  I  C  P  R  N  O  I  R  R
N  A  W  H  E  R  E  I  A  R  B  E  I
C  R  T  E  A  C  H  E  R  S  R  A  P
H  T  M  A  T  H  I  N  T  N  A  D  S
S  C  I  E  N  C  E  D  G  O  R  I  P
O  R  E  P  O  R  T  S  C  W  Y  N  E
C  O  M  P  U  T  E  R  S  H  I  G  L
I  W  R  I  T  I  N  G  G  Y  M  P  L
A  S  S  E  M  B  L  I  E  S  A  G  I
L  H  O  M  E  W  O  R  K  O  H  Y  N
S  T  U  D  I  E  S  H  O  W  L  M  G
```

Teachers
Report
Reading
Computers
Math
Homework
Science
Library
Social Studies
Lunch
Gym
Friends
Art
Assemblies
Music
Where
Writing
Go
Recess
Oh
Field Trips
Why
Spelling
No
How

SAYING GOOD-BYE

Scripture: John 14:1-4

Explain that we are saying good-bye to someone special. Explain why this person is leaving. Ask the children if they have ever had a friend or family member move away. Ask them if and how they keep in touch with friends who have moved away. Remind the children that God is with people when they leave us, and that God has prepared something new for them (new job, new home, new school, new friends, new opportunities and experiences).

Remind children that something new is waiting to happen for us too. We can look forward to experiencing something new too.

☀ Ideas ☀

1. This worship talk can be adapted to a variety of situations (moving, a new school, and so forth).
2. Let the children help plan a special celebration for the person who is leaving.
3. Ask the children to draw pictures and write messages to the person who is leaving. Include these in a scrapbook and give it to the person.
4. Design a banner, and invite the children to decorate it. Let them write messages and draw pictures on it and sign their names. Present this banner to the person who is leaving.
5. Create a leaving litany.
6. At the close of your worship time, ask everyone to form a large circle with person(s) who are leaving in the center. Invite each person to say something special (for example, share memories, wish them luck).

Chapter 9: Feelings

Children experience a variety of feelings, such as fear, anger, love, and sadness. At times children are confused by their feelings. Is it okay for me to feel this way? Do other people ever feel this way?

Through these worship talks children can learn that God is with us no matter what we experience and can realize that God understands our feelings.

I'M SCARED!

Scripture: Joshua 1:9

PROP: A teddy bear

TAKE-HOME GIFT: Teddy bear stickers

TELL THE CHILDREN THIS STORY.

Lisa had been invited to spend the night with her best friend, Kathy. The girls were really excited because this would be their first sleep over. They talked about all of the things they would do.

"We can play games and read stories and draw pictures and do all sorts of neat stuff," said Kathy.

"It's going to be great," said Lisa.

It was great. Lisa and Kathy played games; they read stories; they drew pictures and did all sorts of other neat stuff.

"Time for bed," said Mrs. Henderson.

Lisa and Kathy got into bed. Mrs. Henderson read them a bedtime story. It wasn't even a scary story. Then, Mrs. Henderson kissed both girls good night, turned out the light, and left the room.

"I'll leave the door open and the hall light on," she said.

That's when Lisa got scared. She started to cry.

"Lisa, what's wrong?" asked Kathy.

"I'm scared," wailed Lisa.

"What are you scared of?" asked Kathy.

Lisa just cried. Mrs. Henderson came into the room.

"I want to go home," cried Lisa.

Nothing Mrs. Henderson or Kathy said made Lisa feel better. Finally, Mrs. Henderson called Lisa's mom and told her what was going on. Soon, Lisa's dad came to take her home.

Kathy was crying too, because she didn't want Lisa to go home. Her mom took her on her lap.

"Honey, Lisa has never slept away from home before. She got scared and wanted her parents," her mother said.

"But I spend the night away from home, and I don't get scared," said Kathy. "I just take my teddy bear with me. I say my prayers and then I go to sleep. No one ever had to call you to come and take me home."

"I know, but Lisa is different from you," said her mom. "When people are afraid, we have to be patient with them. Soon they will feel less afraid and be able to do what they were afraid to do."

Kathy thought about what her mother had said. She remembered the story she learned in Sunday school about how the disciples were trying to sleep in a boat. There was a big storm and the disciples were afraid, but Jesus woke up and stopped the storm. He told the disciples that he was right there with them. He told them they didn't have to be afraid that he would go off and leave them alone.

Kathy looked at her mom and said, "You know Brownie, my teddy bear. He kind of reminds me of God. He always has his arms out ready for a big hug. That's how God is, always ready to give us a big hug, especially when we are afraid."

"You are absolutely right. God is always ready to give us a great big hug when we feel scared."

The next day, Kathy went to Lisa's house.

"I'm sorry you got scared last night. Whenever I get scared, I hug my teddy bear real tight. He reminds me of God. His arms are stretched out ready for a hug. That's how God is. His arms are always stretched out and ready to give us a hug," said Kathy.

"Can I stay at your house next Saturday night? I'll bring my teddy bear this time," said Lisa.

"Sure," said Kathy.

On Saturday night, Lisa took her teddy bear and went to Kathy's house. When it was time to go to sleep, both girls hugged their teddy bears and prayed to God.

"Please let Lisa know that you are right here with us as we sleep tonight. Hug both of us real hard and hold us tight while we sleep. Amen." said Kathy.

"Hey, Kathy! Wake up! It's morning! I slept all night and I didn't get scared!" said Lisa.

Remind the children that it is okay to feel afraid. God understands. Say: **God is always with us.**

WILL YOU STILL LOVE ME?

Scripture: John 15:9

TELL THIS STORY.

One day my friend Erin and I were playing at her house. While our parents were inside the house, we decided to swing on the branches of the weeping willow tree. We'd been told never to do that, but we did it anyway. One of the big branches broke off.

"Oh, no!" exclaimed Erin. "We're really going to get it now! Let's not tell. Maybe they won't notice."

We went over to the garage where Erin's brother Mike was playing. He was on top of the roof of the garage with his sled.

"Hey, come on up here!" he said. "It's fun to sled from here and land in the snowbank."

We climbed up on the roof and took turns sledding off the roof. It was fun until the sled fell through the roof with Mike on it. You should have seen the hole in that roof, and the big dent in the roof of the car.

"Boy are we in trouble now," said Mike. "Tell you what, let's keep it a secret."

"I've got an idea. Let's see how high we can throw snowballs," I said.

"Okay!" said Erin and Mike.

We took charcoal and drew black lines on the side of the storage shed. We kept throwing snowballs higher and higher until I threw one right through the window.

"Oops!" I said. "Let's not tell anyone."

"Okay," said Mike.

"Kids, it's time to come in for lunch!" called Erin's mom.

"Coming!" we yelled.

"Now remember, not a word about anything," cautioned Mike.

"You kids sure are quiet," said my mom as we ate lunch.

"Mom, do parents love their kids even if they do bad things?" asked Mike.

"What kind of bad things?" asked my dad.

"Let's say a kid climbed a tree and broke a branch," said Erin.

"Well, that kid would have to cut up the branch and put it with the firewood. That kid would also have to promise never to climb the tree again.

But, yes, I think that kid's parents would still love her," answered Mrs. Carter.

"What if some kids were sledding off the roof of the garage and fell through the roof and left a big hole in the roof and a big dent in the top of the car?" asked Mike.

"That kid would have to pay for the roof and car to be repaired. That kid wouldn't be allowed to sled for a long time. But, yes, that kid's parents would still love him," said Mr. Carter.

"What if some kids used charcoal to draw lines on the side of the white wood shed and threw snowballs at them and broke a window?" I asked.

"That kid would have to pay for a new window and wash the shed," said my dad.

"Yes, and that kid would be grounded for an entire weekend," added my mom.

"What kids did all of these things?" asked Mrs. Carter.

We looked at each other.

"We did," we said.

Our parents took us outside so we could show them what we had done. Just as they said, we had to chop up wood and pay for all the repairs. In the spring we would have to wash the shed and repaint it! None of us was going to have any money left after we paid to repair the window, the roof, and the car. Plus we were all grounded.

"We are very angry with you!" said my parents.

"And sad that you disobeyed us," said Mr. Carter.

"And very, very disappointed in you," said Mrs. Carter.

"But, we still love you and we will always love you," said my parents as they gave me a hug.

"Yes, we do still love you, and we forgive you," said Mrs. Carter.

"Does this mean God doesn't love us anymore?" I asked.

"God loves you very much. God loves all of you no matter what you do."

"Should we tell God we're sorry?" I suggested.

"That's a good idea," said my dad.

We all went inside and sat around the table. We took turns telling God that we were sorry. We asked God to help us not to disobey again. And you can be sure we didn't do any of those things ever again.

 VARIATION

Ask the children to face the congregation. Say to the congregation:

I'm going to ask those of you who are parents to stand up only **if you love your children.** (Parents stand.)

That's a good sign. Your parents love you.

If your children have ever done anything to make you feel sad, angry, or disappointed with them, please raise your hand. (Some parents may raise both hands.)

Well, I guess we've all done some things that make our parents feel sad, angry, or disappointed. You can put your hands down now. Now, if you still love your children, even after they have done something to make you feel sad, angry, or disappointed, please sit down. (The parents will sit down.)

That's a good sign. Our parents still love us even when we have done something wrong.

Ask the children to face you, then tell the preceding story.

I'M SO MAD!

Scripture: Ephesians 4:26

"This has been the worst day of my life!" screamed Beth as she stormed into the house, slamming the door behind her.

Beth flung her books at the wall and tossed her coat on the floor. The cat was in her way, so she shoved him aside with her foot.

"Beth, what in the world is wrong?" asked her mother.

"I'm mad!" shouted Beth.

"I can see that. Tell me what happened," said her mom.

"NO!" yelled Beth as she stormed out of the room.

She shoved her brother, Tim, into the wall as she passed.

"Hey, what did you do that for? I didn't do anything!" said Tim.

"Elizabeth Marie! Stop that this instant!" said her mother. "Calm down and tell me what happened. I'll do whatever I can to help you, but you have to tell me what is wrong."

Beth and her mother sat down.

"You know that report I worked so hard on? On the way to school, Robert grabbed it, ripped it up, and threw it on the ground. When I got to school, and Mrs. Lewis asked for our reports, I told her what happened, but she didn't believe me. She won't let me do it over, so I got a zero on it. Mom, it's not fair. I worked hard on that report," cried Beth.

"Do you know why Robert destroyed it?" asked her mother.

"No. He's always doing things like that. He does it to other kids too, but he never gets in trouble," said Beth.

"It sounds to me like Robert is very unhappy about something. When people are unhappy, sometimes they do things to hurt other people. Let me call Robert's mother and see what I can find out. I'll also call your teacher and explain what happened. Maybe that will help. Is there anything else?"

"Yeah! You know that math test we had last week? Well, I flunked it. I studied. Honest, I did, but I just didn't understand it," cried Beth.

"Beth, sometimes we fail no matter how hard we try, but let's see about getting you some extra help with math. Anything else?" asked her mother.

"Well," said Beth. "Dawn is having a sleep over, and I didn't get invited."

"That feels bad, doesn't it? I can see why you are upset. Did you talk to Dawn about it?" asked her mother.

Just then the phone rang. "It's for you, Beth," said Tim. Beth went to the phone. When she hung up, she was smiling.

"That was Dawn. She wanted to know if I'm coming to her sleep over. I told her that I didn't think I was invited. She said she sent the invitations out two weeks ago and wondered why I hadn't said anything. Do you think maybe my invitation got lost in the mail?"

"I bet it did," said her mother. "Beth, I'm going to call Robert's mother and see if we can find out why he is doing these things. Then I'll call your teacher and see what can be done about your report and your math test."

"Beth, Robert's dad is very sick. They aren't sure if he is going to live. Robert is probably feeling sad and frightened. His mother said she would talk to him, said her mother."

Next, Beth's mom called Mrs. Lewis. She didn't know Robert's dad was so sick. She agreed to let Beth turn the report in on Monday. She also agreed to help Beth with her math after school.

"Beth, I think things are all straightened out," said her mother. "You know, honey, there are things that upset us. It's okay to feel angry. But we can never let our anger cause us to hurt people or damage things. Can you think of some other ways to handle anger?"

"Maybe, I could pound my pillow instead of slamming doors," suggested Beth. "And instead of shoving Tim and the cat, I could have told you that I was angry," said Beth.

"Those are good solutions," said her mother. "Beth, when something happens to upset you, talk to Dad or me. We care about you, and we will try to help you."

"Thanks, Mom," said Beth as she reached over to give her mother a hug. "I'm really sorry about how I acted."

"Forgiven," said her mother. "Beth do you know who else is here to help you?"

Beth paused a moment.

"Yes, I do. God is here to help me, and I bet if I ask, God will help me when I feel angry," said Beth.

"I know God will help you," said her mother.

Encourage the children to think of ways to express their anger. Remind them that God understands our anger and wants to help us with it.

ART: HOW DO I FEEL?

 Draw in faces that show how you sometimes feel.

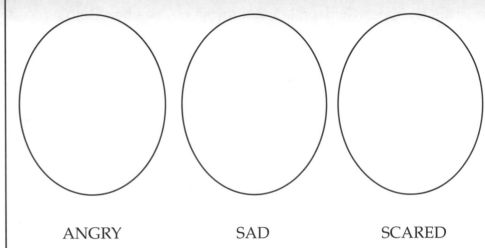

ANGRY   SAD   SCARED

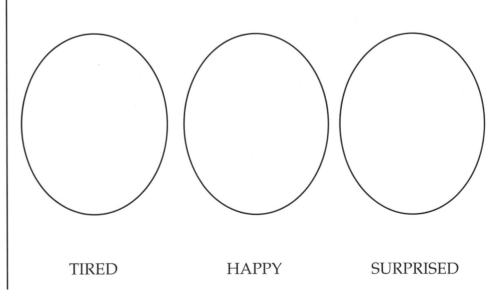

TIRED   HAPPY   SURPRISED

PUZZLE: HOW DO I FEEL?

 Follow the letter path to find these words. Circle each word. The letters in between spell out an important message.

Angry	Happy	Furious	Jealous	Shy
Scared	Joyful	Delighted	Envy	Brave
Surprise	Sad	Concerned	Nervous	Courageous
Worried	Terrified	Excited	Afraid	Cheerful
Glad	Unhappy	Dislike	Content	Solemn
Serious	Loving	Mad		

ANGRYCHAPPYRSURPRISEEEXCITEDAJOYFULFURIOUSONERVOUSRCONCERNEDCDISLIKEHENVYRCONTENTISOLEMNSWORRIEDTAFRAIDAGLADNSERIOUSDBRAVELCHEERFULOSHYVTERRIFIEDIJEALOUSNSCAREDGSADSUNHAPPYPCOURAGEOUSILOVINGRMADIDELIGHTEDT

_ _ _ _ (O) _ _

_ _ (O)(O) _ _ _ _ _ _ — _

_ _ _ _ (O) _ _

_ _ (O) _ _ (O).

The circled letters

spell __ __ __ __ __ __Y

Part 3: WORSHIP SERVICES

Worshiping with children is a joyful and uplifting experience. Children are filled with enthusiasm and energy which allows them to "make a joyful noise to the Lord."

This section includes five worship services for use with children ages 3-10. The stories and music suggested in the "SOMETHING SPECIAL" boxes will enhance your worship experiences. These services are intended for use in children's church. When creating your own worship services, combine the ideas found here with your own ideas and ideas found in Parts 1 and 2 of this book.

Worshiping our Lord with children is exciting and enjoyable. You will share moving times, humorous incidents, and memorable moments. Now, go "make a joyful noise to the LORD all the earth. Worship the LORD with gladness; come into [God's] presence with singing." (Psalm 100:1-2)

☀ Hints ☀

1. If you have a worship team, meet with everyone prior to the service, so that each person knows what to do. This allows you to address questions and concerns worship assistants may have. Include a time of prayer together.
2. Enlist the aid of high school students. They make wonderful assistants.
3. Ask some of the children to say prayers or be the leader in responsive activities.
4. Have a "Children's Sunday." Let the children present the worship service.

PARTS OF A WORSHIP SERVICE

A worship service consists of individual parts that when combined help make up a complete worship service.

Call to Worship

This comes at the beginning of a worship service. It opens the service and lets us know it is time to begin worship. It gets us "warmed up for church."

Musical Responses

This short song that comes before or after the Call to Worship is also called an *Introit*, which means "invitation." We are "inviting" people to worship the Lord with us.

Prayers

Prayers are the words we say to God. They can give thanks or ask God to help us. We can pray for other people, and we can pray for things that concern us.

Prayer Responses

These are either spoken or sung. A spoken prayer response can be a line that the children say after a portion of the prayer is offered. You can use the same response throughout the entire prayer, or you can use a different response.

A musical prayer response comes after the spoken prayer. Music is another way of praying to God.

You can also use a musical prayer prior to beginning a spoken prayer. This is known as a "Call to Prayer." It asks us to get ready to talk to God.

Litany

A litany is a group of thoughts connected by a responsive line. Sometimes the response stays the same and sometimes it differs.

Message

These are sermons that bring a special message to the congregation. They help teach something important about Christians and their faith. They assist us in learning how to live as good Christians. Sometimes stories are used to present the message. Jesus often told stories as a way of teaching.

Music

We praise God by singing songs. We can sing as an entire group. The word *hymn* is sometimes used to speak of music that is sung by the congregation.

Music can be presented by a choir. The music a choir sings is usually referred to as an *anthem*. The words in an anthem are often taken from or inspired by Scripture. Sometimes people sing a solo (alone), a duet (two people) or in other small groups. At other times people play an instrument for worship. The Psalms speak of people praising God with instruments.

Affirmations

An affirmation of faith tells us what we believe about God and Jesus. Affirmations can be spoken or sung.

Benediction

This ends the worship service.

PUZZLE: WHAT ARE WE DOING?

 Connect the dots to find things we do in church.

PRAY

SING

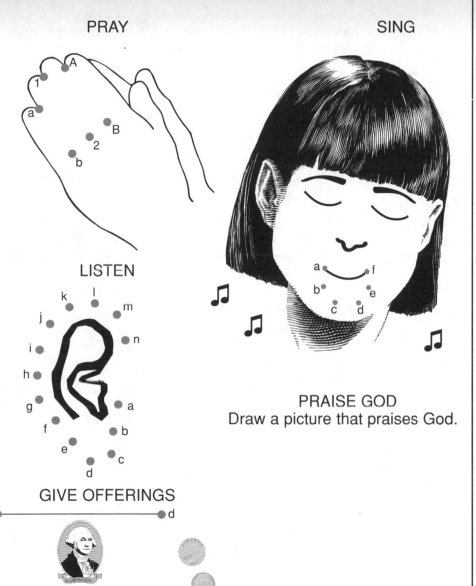

LISTEN

PRAISE GOD
Draw a picture that praises God.

GIVE OFFERINGS

PUZZLE: WHAT'S IN A WORSHIP SERVICE?

Match the parts of the worship service with the correct definition. Write the numbers in the correct spaces.

1. CALL TO WORSHIP ____ These are the gifts we offer to God.

2. INTROIT ____ This closes the worship service.

3. PRAYERS ____ This tells what we believe about God.

4. LITANY ____ These are songs we sing in church.

5. SERMON ____ These are the things we say to God. We use them to thank God and to ask God for help.

6. MUSIC ____ This opens church. It is an invitation to worship God. It gets us "warmed up for church."

7. AFFIRMATION ____ This is a series of thoughts about God. It has a responsive line.

8. OFFERINGS ____ This is a musical invitation that opens church.

9. BENEDICTIONS ____ This is a message that teaches us how to be good Christians.

Theme Sharing and Giving Thanks

Scripture Psalm 100:3-4, Acts 20:35

Materials/Preparation

Beanbags, masking tape

God's Blessings: Select one appropriate to your service

   (a) Outline of tree and branches without leaves drawn on large sheet of white construction paper

   (b) one large brown, construction paper cornucopia per person, one envelope of magazine photos of things we are thankful for per person—cut these into circles (food, family, friends, toys, books, pets) glue sticks, crayons, markers, pencils, notebook paper, colored construction paper

Fill It Up: One large laundry basket, bushel basket, or grocery cart; blindfold; audio cassette of children's Christian songs; audio cassette player. Have the children bring nonperishable food.

Gathering/Opening

• Welcome everyone and let them know that you are thankful they came. Tell them that you are here to give thanks to God.

Exploring Activities

• Say a beanbag prayer. As the children toss the beanbag to one another, ask them to tell something they are thankful about.

• Tell the story of Thanksgiving to the children.

• Read the scripture verses Psalm 100:3-4, Acts 20:35

Message

• Talk about Thanksgiving and why we give thanks. Let the children share their thoughts and feelings. Ask them to tell about how they feel when someone thanks them for something they

※ Idea ※

You can offer this service any time of the year or as a Thanksgiving service in November. If you decide to have a Thanksgiving service, have it in connection with a "Thanksgiving Feast." Invite parents and friends to come to a potluck meal hosted by the children.

have done. Let them share their experiences of times when they haven't been thanked. Talk about why it is important to give thanks and to share what we have with others.

 SOMETHING SPECIAL

Tell the story *Stone Soup* by Marcia Brown. Use props. Give each child a small stone as a reminder to share.

Responding Activities

• *God's Blessings Project:* Give each child a tree/cornucopia, an envelope of pictures, and a glue stick. Let them glue the pictures to the branches of the tree or inside the cornucopia. Pass out paper and pencils to the older children and let them write stories and poems about God's blessings, sharing, and so forth. Let them draw pictures to illustrate their stories and poems. They can glue these to large pieces of construction paper.

※ Hint ※

1. Respect the wishes of those children who prefer not to be blindfolded.

2. Very young children may find it easier just to take an item and place it in the container.

Sharing Our Gifts

• Play "Fill It Up." Put the laundry basket, bushel basket, or grocery cart in the center of your worship area or in an easy-to-reach spot. Play the audio tape of children's songs. Blindfold each child, one at a time. Give each child one of the nonperishable food items. Turn the child around three times, and point him or her in the direction of the container. Let the child place the object in the container. Continue until everyone has had a turn.

Closing

• Give thanks to God.

Theme Celebrating Advent

Scripture Isaiah 40:3

Materials/Preparation

All Weeks: Matches for lighting the Advent Wreath, green hand-shaped cutouts, pencils, glue or tape. Advent wreath set up in the worship area, one gift bag per child to be given out the week before Advent.

Week 1

Advent Wreath: One green circular piece of craft foam per child, three purple candles, one pink candle, one free-standing white candle, pieces of artificial evergreen, poinsettias and holly, one piece of heavy duty white poster board (14" square) per child, glue guns and glue

Week 2 Manger scene set up in your worship area (Try to use a large scene.)

Christmas Cards: Green, red, and white construction paper (8" x 10"); green, red, silver and gold glitter; glue; crayons; Christmas stickers; envelopes

Week 3 Undecorated, artificial Christmas tree set up in your worship area.

Christmas Mural: 1 piece of white construction paper (12" x 18") per child, red and green crayons, red and green glitter, glue, tape, cutouts of Christmas objects (stars, poinsettias, wreaths, trees, candy canes, wise men, camels, donkey, Mary, Joseph, Jesus, shepherds). These can be cut from Christmas wrapping

> ### ✳ Hint ✳
> This is intended to be a series of four services to be held during the Advent season. Try to have a special service for children each week of Advent. There will be different activities at each weekly service.

paper, Christmas cards or magazines. One envelope per child. Put a variety of Christmas cutouts into each envelope.

Week 4 Grocery cart and poinsettias set up in the worship area

Play Dough Ornaments: Red, green, and white play dough (Mix 1 cup flour, 1 cup salt, and 1/2 cup water. Add a few drops of vegetable oil if desired. Add additional water or flour to get proper consistency. Add green tempera to one batch and red tempera to one batch. Leave one batch white.); red, green, and white glitter; glue; Christmas cookie cutters; pencil with eraser; red, green and white yarn cut into 6" pieces; rolling pins, one paper lunch sack per child (Print each child's name on their sack.); paper towels; plastic bags

Gathering/Opening

- Welcome everyone and tell them that we are going to get ready to celebrate the birth of Jesus. Remind them that God sent Jesus to be our friend, helper, and savior.
- Light the Advent Wreath (Select a different child to light it each week.)

Week 1: Say: **The first candle on the Advent Wreath is the candle of promise. It reminds us that God promised to send his son Jesus to earth. Jesus came to help us learn about God. The Advent Wreath is green to remind us that God promises us everlasting life if we accept Christ as our savior. It is round to remind us that God promises to always love us.**

Week 2: Say: **Today we light the candle of hope. Jesus came to bring hope into the world. We hope that we can make the world a better place by doing good things and by helping other people. God hopes that we will accept Jesus as Lord and Savior.**

Week 3: Say: **Today, we light the candle of peace. Jesus came to bring peace into the world. God does not want us to fight with each other. God wants us to live in peace.**
Week 4: Say: **Today we light the candle of joy. Jesus will bring joy into our lives. God wants us to be joyful. We can praise God with joy and happiness.**

Exploring Activities

• Say a "Give Me a Hand" prayer. Give each child a green hand cutout and a pencil. Let the children write a prayer on the handprint. One at a time, each child can share his or her prayer. Make the handprints into a wreath.

Message

Each week tell a different part of the Christmas story.

• •

 SOMETHING SPECIAL

Each week share a different story.
Week 1: "The City that Forgot About Christmas" by Mary Warren in *Christmas Classics for Children*
Week 2: *All Those Mothers at the Manger* by Norma Farber
Week 3: "Little Tree and His Wish" by Viola Ruiz in *Christmas Classics for Children*
Week 4: "The Mysterious Star" by Joanne Marxhausen in *Christmas Classics for Children*

• •

Responding Activities
Week 1
• Sing the first verse of "O Come All Ye Faithful."
• Make an Advent Wreath. Give each person the materials. Show the children how to use the pencil erasers to poke holes in the foam. Insert the three purple candles and the pink candle. Put glue around the candles at the insertion point. Glue the wreath to the cardboard. Glue the white candle in the center of the

wreath. Glue the holly, evergreen, and poinsettias around the wreath to decorate it. Label with each child's name. Let them take these home. Tell them to light their wreath each day and say a prayer.

Week 2
• Sing the first verse of "Hark, the Herald Angels Sing"
• Make Christmas cards. Give the children the materials. Let them fold their paper any way they choose. Tell them to decorate their papers and make them into Christmas cards. Send the cards to people on your church prayer list.

Week 3
• Sing the first verse of "Silent Night."
• Make a Christmas mural. Give each child a piece of paper. Set the decorating materials out on the table. Tell the children to decorate their paper any way they want. Have them write a greeting and sign their name. Use tape to join the papers together to make a mural. Hang it in the hall where all can enjoy it.

Week 4
• Sing the first verse of "Joy to the World."
• Make play dough ornaments. Give each child a piece of play dough. Help the children to roll out the dough. Show them how to use the cookie cutters to make ornaments. Each child can make two or three ornaments. Use a pencil eraser to poke a hole in the top of each child's ornament. Put the yarn through the hole and tie at the top. Let the children use the glitter and glue to decorate their ornaments. Label the ornaments with their names and let dry. Help the children to wrap the ornaments in paper towels and put them into their paper bags. Tell the parents to let these dry overnight before hanging them on the tree.

SOMETHING SPECIAL

Have your children's choir or the entire group sing "Come Lord Jesus" each week. It is in the book *Hi God, 2.*
Other songs they can sing over the years include "Violet in the Snow" from *Hi God, 2;* "What Can We Give to the King" from *The Birthday Party;* "When God Becomes a Baby" from *Hark, the Herald Angel*

Sharing Our Gifts

Week 1: The week before Advent, give each child a gift bag. Ask them to fill it with items for a boy or a girl. Items can include paperback book, crayons, coloring books, age-appropriate games or toys, toothpaste, toothbrush, comb, or other small items. Have them label the bag indicating the gender and age of the child the bag is intended for. Have them bring these to the first service. Distribute them to an agency that works with needy families.

Week 2: Ask each child to bring a new or gently used stuffed animal. Add it to your manger scene. Donate these to the hospital to give to children who come into the emergency room.

Week 3: Ask each child to bring mittens, hat, or scarf for a child. Hang these on the undecorated Christmas tree. Donate them to needy children.

Week 4: Ask each child to bring baby food, disposable diapers, bottles, or other small baby items. Give them to the local food pantry to distribute to needy families.

Each week put a bushel basket, grocery cart or other container in the worship area. Have the children place their items in the container. The stuffed animals may be added to the manger scene.

Closing

• Let us remember to share the good news with the world.

Take home activities

• Give each child a sheet of paper asking them to bring something for the offering each week (*Week before Advent:* Return the gift bag for next week; *Week 1:* Small stuffed animal for next week; *Week 2:* A pair of mittens, a hat, or a scarf for a child; *Week 4:* Baby item (disposable diapers, jar of baby food, bottles) for next week.

Worship Service 3: A Friend Is

Theme Friendship

Scripture John 15:15

Materials/Preparation

Friends: Encourage children to bring a friend.

Sharing Our Gifts: Audio cassette of Christian children's songs and cassette player.

A Sweet Treat: Several batches of your favorite sugar cookie dough, cookie cutters in a variety of shapes, cookie decorating sprinkles and gels, rolling pins, preheated oven, timer, flour, paper, pencils, cookie trays, metal spatula. Roll out the cookie dough.

Cards: Colored construction paper, crayons, markers, pencils

A Friendship Mural: Instant camera and film, glue, long piece of white paper, crayons, markers, pencils, glue

Friendship Commitments: Index cards, pencils

Gathering/Opening

- Welcome everyone and tell them that Jesus wants to be their friend. Explain that God sent Jesus to be our friend and to teach us how to live as good Christians.

Exploring Activities

- Create a litany about friendship.
- Share scripture verses on friendship: John 15:15, James 2:23

Message

- Talk about friendship. Discuss what being a good friend means.

※ Hint ※

1. For large groups, divide the children into smaller groups. Have one basket per group.
2. Have extra change on hand for those who forget their offering.

SOMETHING SPECIAL

Share the story, *A Friend Is Someone Who Likes You* by Joan Walsh Anglund. Make this into a flannelboard story. Make the pieces large.

Responding Activities

- Do a service project called *A Sweet Treat*. Have each child cut out and decorate two cookies. Make note of where each person's cookies are. Bake the cookies. Decorate cookies when they are cool. Eat them! Deliver some to homebound members.
- Make get-well cards or thinking-of-you cards for friends who are ill. Make a large "Friendship Mural." Take instant photos of the children. Have the children draw friendship pictures and write friendship thoughts. Glue their photos to the mural. Give these murals to children who are homebound.
- Make "Friendship Commitments." Have each child write their "friendship commitment" on an index card. Let the children take their cards home and work on their commitment.
- Have the children write stories, songs, and poems about friendship.

Sharing Our Gifts

- Have the children sit on the floor in a circle. Play a tape of children's Christian songs. Pass the offering basket around the circle. Stop the music. The child holding the basket deposits his/her offering and leaves the circle. Continue until all children have added their money.

Closing

- Let one of the children offer this: *"God, thank you for our friends. Help us to be friendly to everyone we meet. Amen!"*

Worship Service 4: Love One Another

Theme Learning About Christian Love

Scripture John 13:35 and John 15:9

Materials/Preparation
Meal: Heart-shaped cookies, sandwiches, fruit molds, cakes, red and pink juices, red fruits, red and pink paper goods
Prayer Vine: Trellis standing against a wall, pre-cut leaves, tape
Making Valentines: Pink, red, white construction paper hearts in a variety of sizes; red and pink glitter; crayons and markers; pencils; glue
Love Is: One large sheet of white construction paper per person, pink and red crayons, markers and pencils, staples and stapler

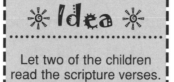

❋ Idea ❋

Let two of the children read the scripture verses.

Gathering/Opening
• Welcome everyone and let them know that God loves them. Tell them that today you will be learning about the love God has for us and how God wants us to share that love with others.

Exploring Activities
• Say a Prayer Vine Prayer. Ask each child to write a prayer on a leaf. Let each person offer their prayer as they add their leaf to the vine on the trellis.
    • Share scripture verses about love. John 13:35, John 15:9 (and others if desired)

❋ Hint ❋

Consider having this service in connection with Valentine's Day. Have a family meal. Let the children act as hosts to their parents and other invited guests.

Message
• Talk about God's love for us. Talk about parents loving their children. Ask the children to share their thoughts on love. **How do we show love for each other?**

 SOMETHING SPECIAL

Share the story *Love Is a Special Way of Feeling* by Joan Walsh Anglund. Since the pictures are small, make this into story cards. Enlarge the pictures and glue them to construction paper.

Responding Activities
• Sing "Jesus Loves Me."
• Make Valentines. Let the children use the pre-cut hearts, glitter, crayons, markers, and glue to make dozens and dozens of Valentines. Give these to church staff members, each other, family members, hospitalized/homebound church members, and keep some for yourself.
• Do a church service project. Make a book, "Love is . . ." Give each child a piece of white construction paper. Tell them to print "Love Is" across the top. (Do this for younger children.) Have them draw a picture of what love means to them. (Love is giving hugs. Love is helping other people.) Have them complete the sentence and write it across the bottom of their picture. Ask two children to design a front and back cover. Put the pages together, add the covers, staple the book together, and put the book into your church library.

Sharing Our Gifts
• Play a tape of quiet, instrumental music. Pass the offering basket and let the children add their offerings. Tell the children this is a time when they can pray silently to God. Let the music play for a minute or two after all of the money has been collected.

Closing (Let one of the children say this.)
Loving God, let us show our love for you this week. Help us to show our love for other people, for our families, for our teachers, and for our friends. Thank you for loving us so much. AMEN.

Worship Service 5: God's Creation

Theme Celebrating God's Creation

Scripture Genesis 1–2:3

Materials/Preparation

"Bounce and Roll Prayers"—One large ball

"What in the World?"—Several sheets of black and white construction paper, cutouts of clouds, sun, moon, stars, animals, fish, birds, flowers, rainbows, rain, snow, lakes, rivers, mountains, and forth; blindfold, audio cassette of children's music, cassette player, copies of the activities listed at the end. Tape the black pieces of paper together. Tape the white pieces of paper together. Tape both to the wall alongside one another at child height. Put the cutouts into a box.

"God Created"—Heavy, light blue construction paper; heavy, dark blue construction paper; colored tissue paper; crayons; glue; shaving cream. Cut the tissue paper into squares and circles.

✳ Hint ✳

This worship service can become several services. If you choose to highlight creation, you can have one service for each day of creation. This would make a wonderful vacation Bible school experience. You can also use it to highlight the seasons. Have one **God's Creation** worship service for each season.

Gathering/Opening

• Welcome everyone and let them know that each person is special and created in God's image. God's image is good, which means that each person is good. Tell the children that today you will be celebrating Creation.

• Sing "God Created" to the tune of "Twinkle, Twinkle Little Star."

God created day and night.

The sun and stars and moonlight.

God created birds and fish.

God created animals.

God created land, sky, sea.

And God created you and me!

✳ Hint ✳

1. Create verses that highlight the seven days of creation.
2. Create a song to highlight each season.

Exploring Activities

• Say a bounce-and-roll prayer. Form a circle. Have each child bounce or roll a ball to someone else while giving thanks for something God has created.

• Use a children's Bible to tell the Creation story. Make this into a flannelboard.

Message

• If you are highlighting the Creation story, talk about each of the things God created on that day. **Why did God create them? Why are they needed?**

• If you are highlighting the seasons, talk about the season we are in. **What is special about it? What makes it different from the other seasons? Why did God create a world with seasons? Why is the name of each season special?**

SOMETHING SPECIAL

If you are highlighting Creation, use one of these stories.
The Dreamer by Cynthia Rylant, *And God Created Squash* by Martha Whitmore Hickman, *Old Turtle* by Douglas Wood, *Designed by God, So I Must Be Special* by Bonnie Sose, *The World God Made* by Donna Cooner

If you are highlighting the seasons, use a seasonal story
The Friendly Snowflake by M. Scott Peck (Winter), *Spring Is a New Beginning* by Joan Walsh Anglund (Spring), *The Summer Night* by Charlotte Zolotow (Summer), *Say It!* by Charlotte Zolotow (Autumn)

Responding Activities

- Play "What in the World?" Show the children the mural that is on the wall. Show them the box of cutouts. Tell them you are going to "create the world." Play the music tape. Blindfold each child, one at a time. Let each child reach into the box and pull out a cutout. Turn the child around three times and point him/her toward the mural. Let the child find a place to put the item. When everyone has had a turn, take a good look at the world you created. Who did a better job? You or God? Discuss this with the children.

- Have each child draw a picture of something God created. They can highlight the day of creation or the season.

- Do a "God Created" art project.

In Winter give each child a piece of blue construction paper and some shaving cream. Let them fingerpaint a "snowy picture."

In Spring or Summer give each child a piece of blue paper, green, yellow, pink, and purple tissue paper; glue; and crayons. Let the children create spring or summer picture.

In Autumn give each child a piece of light blue construction paper and brown crayons. Have them turn their paper length-wise. Have them use the brown crayon to draw a tree trunk and branches. Give them precut squares of red, orange, and yellow tissue paper. Show them how to squish the tissue and glue it to the tree branches and to the ground under the tree.

For Days of Creation adapt this project accordingly. Let the children use a variety of art materials to highlight each day of creation. Join each picture together in the proper order to make a "creation mural."

Sharing Our Gifts

- Find a tape of environmental music or sounds. Play this as you collect their offerings. Let the children have a few moments to sit quietly and listen to the sounds of nature.

Closing

(Ask a child to say this.)

Thank you God for creating this beautiful world for us. Help us to take good care of our world. Help us to show others how to care for our world. In the name of the Creator, Christ, and Loving Spirit. AMEN.

Appendix

Appendix:

USING FLANNELBOARDS

BEFORE YOU BEGIN

Make a large flannelboard for use in telling stories. You will need a sturdy stand capable of supporting the flannelboard. This portable flannelboard can be moved into the worship area to use during worship talks.

FLANNELBOARD MATERIALS

one large piece of wood or heavy-duty foam board. The board should measure 3 feet by 2 feet or larger.
large piece of pale gray Velcro attracting material. The material should be large enough to cover both sides of the board.

A ready-made board can be ordered from
Charles Mayer Studios Inc.
168 E. Market St.
Akron, OH 44308
This is well constructed and will last for many years.

DIRECTIONS

1. Use heavy-duty glue (or a glue gun) to attach material to the board. An option is to have the material one inch larger than the board. Place the two pieces together so that the pieces are inside out. Use a sewing machine to stitch around the two pieces of material using a 1/4 inch seam. Leave one end open. Turn the material right side out, slip it over the board, and hand stitch the opening shut.

FIGURE MATERIALS

Velcro (self-stick strips) in the following colors: navy blue, white, beige, red. This can be purchased by the yard in fabric stores.
felt in a variety of colors

several yards of white pellon. Pellon should not be too fleecy (this avoids smearing when coloring figures.) This too can be purchased in fabric stores.

MAKING FLANNELBOARD FIGURES

1. Trace the picture onto the pellon. Color with crayons or markers. Cut out. Glue a small piece of Velcro to the back. Colorful felt with Velcro attached can also be used to make flannelboard figures.

2. Be creative in your use of flannelboard materials. Use animal prints and furs to make animals. Be willing to experiment with angel hair, glitter, sequins, decorative borders and more to add interest to your flannelboard figures.

3. Store flannelboard stories in file pockets. Print the name of each story on the top. List all of the pieces you have inside. Include a copy of the story inside.

4. Attach a book pocket and checkout card to the front of the folder for anyone who uses it.

5. Store flannelboard stories alphabetically by story title.

CREATING STORY CARDS

MATERIALS

pastel colored card or cover stock paper
rubber cement or glue
coloring books and paperback storybooks of Bible stories (Two copies of each are needed so you can use both sides of each page.)
crayons
scissors
marker or computer.

DIRECTIONS

1. If you are using coloring books, color and cut out each picture you will need to use.

2. Glue it to a piece of card or cover stock paper.

3. Hand print or use the computer to type out the text.

4. Glue the appropriate text to the back of each picture.

5. Number the pictures on the back so the story is arranged in the proper order.

6. If you are using paperback picture books, cut out each picture and glue it to the stock paper. Cut out the appropriate text and glue it to the back of the paper. Number the cards on the back, so the story is in the proper order.

7. Store cards in file pockets. Put the title of the story on the pocket and list how many cards are in each pocket

8. Attach a book pocket and checkout card to the front of each folder for anyone who uses it.

9. Store the cards alphabetically by story.

STORYTELLING HINTS

1. Often a story is so good that it can stand on its own without being explained. Refrain from offering an explanation of every story you share with the children. There are times when you can offer a story and dismiss the children with "Thank you for coming."

2. When a book includes outstanding illustrations, share them with the children rather than make a flannelboard version.

3. The use of props and other audio and visual aids can enhance some stories. However, there are times when telling a story without the use of illustrations, props or other aids is best. If the children comment on this, tell them you are going to let them create pictures of the story in their imagination.

4. Allow yourself plenty of preparation time when presenting a worship talk or planning a worship service. You will need time to gather materials, create flannelboard stories and practice. You will also find it easier to locate needed library materials when you start early.

5. Plan a workshop day for those who work in your Christian education program. Choose the stories you want to create flannelboards, story cards, and props for. Have the materials and supplies ready for each project. Assign one or more people to each project. By the end of your workshop, you will have created several items that can be used.

6. Ask for assistance from other members of your congregation. Do you have retired artists, teachers, or tailors in your midst? If so, ask them if they would be willing to help create materials for your program. Many older people who cannot get out much are willing to do work at home if someone brings and picks up the materials.

7. Ask each person who works with your childrens' program to create one thing before the start of each year.

8. Store props in boxes. List the materials on the outside of the box. Put a typed copy of the story inside each box. Attach a book pocket and check out card to each box of props. Have people check these out before they use them.

9. Make a master list of all materials you have for your program.

Resource List

STORY BOOKS

AUTHOR	TITLE
Anglund, Joan Walsh	*A Friend Is Someone Who Likes You* New York: Harcourt, Brace & World, 1983. We have many different kinds of friends. (page 162)
	Love Is a Special Way of Feeling San Diego: Harcourt Brace Jovanovich, 1985. Love makes us feel good. (page 163)
	Spring Is a New Beginning New York: Harcourt Brace Jovanovich, 1963. Spring unfolds and brings new life. (pages 122, 165)
Brown, Marcia.	*Stone Soup.* New York: Scribner, 1947 A town shared what they had and made stone soup. (page 158)
Carle, Eric	*The Mixed-Up Chameleon* New York: HarperCollins Publishers, 1988. Chameleon learned that he was special just the way he was. (page 112)
	Christmas Classics for Children St. Louis: Concordia, 1981. Includes: "The City that Forgot About Christmas" (pages 135, 160), "Little Tree and His Wish" (pages 136 ,160), "The Mysterious Star" (pages 137, 160).

AUTHOR	TITLE
Cooner, Donna	*The World God Made* Waco, Tex.: Word, 1994. (page 165)
de Paola, Tomie	*The Legend of Old Befana* San Diego: Harcourt Brace Jovanovich, 1980. Old Befana was too busy to visit Jesus. (page 139)
Farber, Norma	*All Those Mothers at the Manger* New York: Harper & Row, 1985. There were many mothers at the manger the night Jesus was born. (pages 135, 160)
Heide, Florence P.	*Who Needs Me?* Minneapolis: Augsburg, 1971. A child discovers all those who need him, including God. (page 114)
Hickman, Martha Whitmore	*And God Created Squash* Morton Grove: Albert Whitman & Company, 1996. God created a wonderful world for us. (page 143)
Hunt, Angela Elwell.	*Tale of Three Trees* Batavia, Ill.: Lion Publishing, 1989. The first tree became a manger, the second tree a fishing boat, and the third tree a cross. (page 130)

AUTHOR	TITLE
Lionni, Leo	*A Color of His Own* New York: Alfred A. Knopf, 1993. Chameleon discovered that changing colors made him special. (page 112)
Marxhausen, Joanne	*The Mysterious Star* St. Louis: Concordia, 1974. Jamie helped many people learn about the star. (pages 137, 160)
Peck, M. Scott	*The Friendly Snowflake* Atlanta: Turner Publishing, 1992. A child made friends with a snowflake named Harry. (pages 121, 165)
Pfister, Marcus	*The Christmas Star* New York: North-South Books, 1993. The beautiful star led them to a baby. (page 139)
Rylant, Cynthia	*The Dreamer* New York: Blue Sky Press, 1993. An artist created a beautiful world. (pages 143, 165)
Sechrist, Elizabeth	*It's Time for Easter* Philadelphia: Macrae Smith Co. 1961. Includes: "Even Unto the End of the World." (page 131)
Sose, Bonnie	*Designed by God, So I Must Be Special* Winter Park: Character Builders for Kids, 1991. Each of us is a special part of God's world. (page 165)
Tazewell, Charles	*The Littlest Angel* Chicago: Children's Press, 1991. The little angel gave Jesus a wonderful gift. (page 138)

AUTHOR	TITLE
Waber, Bernard	*You Look Ridiculous, Said the Rhinoceros to the Hippopotamus* Boston: Houghton Mifflin Co., 1973. Everyone told hippopotamus he looked ridiculous, so he changed his appearance. (page 112)
Wood, Douglas	*Old Turtle* Duluth: Pfeifer-Hamilton, 1991. Old Turtle helped settle an argument about God. (pages 143, 165)
Zolotow, Charlotte	*Say It!* New York: Morrow, 1992. The little girl and her mother shared a special time together. (pages 123, 165)
	The Summer Night New York: HarperCollins, 1991. A young girl and her father enjoyed a summer night. (pages 122, 165)

ADDITIONAL RESOURCE

AUTHOR	TITLE
Dingwall, Cindy	*Bible Time With Kids: 400+ Bible-based Activties to Use with Children* Nashville: Abingdon Press, 1997. These lessons and activities can be used with the worship activities presented here.

STORYTELLING RESOURCES

These books provide excellent advise on sharing stories with children.

AUTHOR	TITLE
Bauer, Caroline Feller	*New Handbook for Storytellers* Chicago: American Library Association, 1993.
Bauer, Caroline Feller	*This Way to Books* Bronx: H. W. Wilson, 1983.
Lima, Carolyn	*A to Zoo: Subject Access to Children's Picture Books* New York: Bowker, 1993.

FLANNELBOARD BOOKS

Anderson, Paul S.	*Storytelling with the Flannel Board*. (3 vols.) Minneapolis: T.S. Denison, 1970
Darling, Kathy	*Holiday Hoopla: Flannel Board Fun* Carthage, Ill.: Monday Morning Books/Good Apple, 1990. Order from Good Apple P.O. Box 480 Parsippany, NJ 07054
Sierra, Judy	*The Flannel Board Storytelling Book* Bronx: H.W. Wilson Co., 1987.
Taylor, Frances and Gloria G. Vaughn	*The Flannelboard Storybook* Atlanta: Humanics LTD., 1986.
Warren, Jean	*Mix and Match Series* Everett, Wash.: Warren Publishing House, Inc., 1990. Order from Warren Publishing House P.O. Box 2250 Everett, WA 98202
Wilmes, Liz and Dick	*Felt Board Fun* Elgin, Ill.: Building Blocks, 1984. Order from Building Blocks 3893 Brindlewood Elgin, IL 60123

AUTHOR	TITLE

These companies produce beautiful ready-made flannelboards and backgrounds.
LAKESHORE LEARNING MATERIALS
2695 Dominquez, St. Carson, CA 90749

THE STORYTELLER
308 E. 800 South PO Box 921, Salem, Utah 84653

MUSIC RESOURCES

Black, Charles (arranger)	"The Friendly Beasts" Harold Flammer Inc, 1968. A delightful arrangement for children's choir. (page 138)
Landry, Carey	*Hi God*, 2 Phoenix: North American Liturgy Resources, 1976. The lovely music is arranged for childrens' voices and works well in Sunday school, choir, and VBS. (pages 128, 131, 135, 144, 161)
Long, Ron E. and Joanne Barrett	*Hark, the Herald Angel* Kansas City: Lillenas Publishing Co., 1983. Hark was the angel who had been chosen to deliver the good news about Jesus. (pages 137, 161)
Okan, Milton,	*The Birthday Party* Port Chester: Cherry Lane Music Co., Inc. There is going to be a party for a King! (pages 136, 161)
——.	*Sing 'n' Celebrate for Kids*, vol. 2 Waco, Tex.: Word, 1982. Overflowing with a variety of songs, this book provides music for Sunday school, children's choir and VBS. (pages 113, 134, 141)
Warren, Jean (compiler)	*Piggyback Songs in Praise of God* and *Piggyback Songs in Praise of Jesus*. These songs about God and Jesus are set to familiar tunes. (page 79)

Title and Theme Index

Scripture Index

The scripture index is listed in alphabetical order.

Acts 20:32	73	Isaiah 40:3	159-61	Luke 15:3-6	46-47	Matthew 28:19	94, 141	Psalm 100:4	25, 26, 134
Acts 20:35	158	Isaiah 40:31	127	Luke 19:28-44	129	Matthew 28:20	93	Psalm 100:5	127
				Luke 22:14-20	21, 128			Psalm 102:1	63, 64, 69, 72
Daniel 2:21	123	James 1:17	73, 74	Luke 23	130	Micah 7:7	102		
				Luke 24:1-49	23, 24, 130			Psalm 105:1	25, 26
Ephesians 4:26	151-52	John 3:2	49	Luke 24:36	63	Numbers 6:24-26	94	Psalm 106:1	74, 77, 92
Ephesians 5:1	52	John 3:16	143-44			Numbers 24:17	28	Psalm 107:1	49-50
		John 9:38	55	Mark 1:8	94			Psalm 109:26	63, 84
Exodus 20:1-17	43-44	John 12:36	60-61	Mark 10:14	109	Proverbs 18:24	52	Psalm 111:1	74
Exodus 20:12	75, 76, 131	John 12:46	57	Mark 11:1-11	129	Proverbs 24:32	119	Psalm 118:24	14, 15
Exodus 33:14	93	John 13:35	163	Mark 11:9	22, 98	Proverbs 28:20	82	Psalm 121:2	127
		John 14:1	58	Mark 14:17-25	128	Proverbs 30:5	127	Psalm 130:7	135
1 John 1:9	114	John 14:1-4	146	Mark 15:1-47	130			Psalm 136:1	127
		John 14:27	136	Mark 16	23, 24, 130	Psalm 5:2	72	Psalm 145:8	63
1 Peter 1:25	126, 127	John 15:5	88	Mark 16:15	93, 96, 100	Psalm 9:1	100	Psalm 145:9	63, 86
		John 15:9	52, 149-50			Psalm 9:1-2	100	Psalm 147:16-17	121
1 Thessalonians 5:17	129	John 15:14	42	Matthew 1:18-25	137	Psalm 23	70	Psalm 150:1	63, 84
1 Thessalonians 5:25	82	John 15:15	162	Matthew 1:21	38	Psalm 23:1	127	Psalm 150:3-4	15
		John 18:28–19:42	130	Matthew 1:23	63, 72	Psalm 34:11	13	Psalm 150:3-5	17
Galatians 3:26	61	John 20:1-18	130-31	Matthew 2:2-12	139	Psalm 38:18	116-17		
		John 20–21	23, 24	Matthew 2:7-11	32, 33	Psalm 40:16	14	Revelations 21:5	121-22
Genesis 1:1–2:3	42, 55, 143, 164-65	John 21:15-17	134	Matthew 2:10-11	106	Psalm 46:1	63		
				Matthew 4:19	46	Psalm 47:1	19, 78, 87	Romans 10:9	60
Genesis 1:26-27	112	Joshua 1:9	148-49	Matthew 5:1-12	45	Psalm 55:1	72	Romans 15:33	63
Genesis 8:22	122			Matthew 5:8	127	Psalm 59:16	13		
Genesis 23:6	63	Luke 1:10-14	78	Matthew 21:1-11	129	Psalm 63:4	37	2 Corinthians 9:15	76, 77
Genesis 28:15	91, 93	Luke 2:1-20	50, 137-38	Matthew 21:6-9	22	Psalm 66:1	16		
		Luke 2:7	32, 127	Matthew 21:9	98	Psalm 67:1	92	2 Peter 3:18	113
Hebrews 13:6	54	Luke 2:10	30	Matthew 25:35	17, 68	Psalm 86:12	92		
		Luke 2:10-11	104	Matthew 25:40	115-16	Psalm 88:2	73	Titus 3:15	66
Isaiah 7:14	28, 29, 134-35	Luke 2:10-14	78, 79	Matthew 26:17-29	128	Psalm 92:1	63		
		Luke 2:14	63	Matthew 26:26-27	19, 21, 96	Psalm 96:1	92		
Isaiah 9:6	31	Luke 2:40	68-69, 144	Matthew 27:15-44	130	Psalm 100:1	63		
Isaiah 12:4	63	Luke 4:14-15	40	Matthew 28	23, 24, 130	Psalm 100:2	63, 114		
Isaiah 55:12	136-37	Luke 9:57	54	Matthew 28:6	74, 75	Psalm 100:3-4	158		

Age Index

PRE-SCHOOL/KINDERGARTEN AGES 3-6

ACTIVITIES

TITLE	PAGE #	THEME	TYPE OF ACTIVITY
God's Beautiful World	124	Creation/Seasons	Art
Help the Shepherd Find His Lost Sheep	48	Helping/Lost	Maze
How Do I Feel?	152	Feelings	Art
Jesus Loves Me	37	Love	Art
Jesus Loves You	51	Love	Puzzle
Let's Find Jesus	53	Searching	Maze
What Are We Doing?	157	Worship	Puzzle
What Did They Wear?	35	Epiphany	Puzzle
When We Pray	81	Prayer	Puzzle

AFFIRMATIONS

TITLE	PAGE #	THEME	TYPE OF ACTIVITY
God Is My Friend	52	Friendship	Speak/Movement
God Loves You	52	Love	Speak/Movement
I Love Jesus	52	Love	Speaking
Jesus Helps Us	54	Helping	Speaking
Jesus Is My Friend	42	Friendship	Speak/Movement
Let's Follow Jesus	54	Following	Speak/Movement
What Do I Believe?	60	Creation	Speaking

CALLS TO WORSHIP

TITLE	PAGE #	THEME	TYPE OF ACTIVITY
Come Give Thanks	25	Thanksgiving	Speak/Movement
Come On	13	General	Speak/Movement
Come, Say Thank You	26	Thanksgiving	Music
If You Want to Praise God	19	General	Music/Movement
Good Morning	13	General	Speak/Movement
Good News	23	Easter	Speaking
Let's Get Ready	28	Christmas	Speaking
Lighting the Christ Candle	31	Christmas	Music
Time to Get Ready	30	Advent	Speaking
Time to Light the Advent Wreath	29	Advent	Music
Wise Men, The	33	Epiphany	Drama

LITANIES

TITLE	PAGE #	THEME	TYPE OF ACTIVITY
Jesus Is My Friend	42	Friendship	Music
Let's Go Look for That Sheep	46-47	Searching	Speak/Movement
Let's Follow Jesus	54	Following	Speak/Movement
Who Loves Us?	37	Love	Speak/Movement

PRAYERS

ELEMENTARY—AGES 6-10
ACTIVITIES

AFFIRMATIONS

CALLS TO WORSHIP

TITLE	PAGE #	THEME	TYPE OF ACTIVITY
Listen God	72	General	Music
Lord Hear Us	72	General	Music
New School Year, A	68-69	School	Speaking
Our Gift to You	73	Offering	Speaking
Please Be with Us	72	General	Music
Play Ball	84	General	Speak/Movement
Praise, Praise, Praise the Lord	74	General	Music
Prayer Chains	86	Prayer	Writing/Speaking
Prayer Vine	88	Prayer	Writing/Speaking
Someone Special	70	Death	Speaking
Something Special	73, 79	General	Music
Stand, Clap, and Say Thank You	76	Mother's/Father's Day	Music
Thank You, God	76	Mother's/Father's Day	Music
Thanks, Thanks, Thanks to God	74	Thanksgiving	Music
We Come to Give Our Gifts	73	Offering	Music
We Come to Pray to You Today	73	General	Music
We Give You Our Gifts	73	Offering	Music

TITLE	PAGE #	THEME	TYPE OF ACTIVITY
We Come to Praise the Lord!	75	Easter	Music
Welcome	68	Welcoming	Speaking
Welcome Jesus	78	Christmas	Speaking

WORSHIP TALKS

TITLE	PAGE #	THEME	TYPE OF ACTIVITY
Awesome Autumn	123	Seasons	Participation
Bible Presentation Sunday	126	Bible	Storytelling
Christmas Peace	136	Advent	Participation
Come Be Baptized	141	Baptism	Participation
Coming in Hope	135	Advent	Participation
Coming in Joy	136-37	Advent	Participation
Creation	143	Creation	Participation
Crucify Him	130	Good Friday	Storytelling
Death Brings New Life	143	Death/Resurrection	Participation
Don't Forget Jesus	134	Advent	Participation
God Erases Our Sins	114	Sin	Participation
God Needs Me	114	Self-Esteem	Participation
Happy Birthday, Jesus	138	Christmas	Drama
Happy New School Year	144	School	Participation
Happy Mother's/Father's Day	131	Mothers/Fathers Day	Participation

Puzzle Solutions:

JESUS LOVES YOU p.18

WELCOME

WORSHIPING GOD p.20

```
C L A P HANDS
I N S T R U M E N T S
    D A N C I N G
T H A N K S G I V I N G
        S H O U T I N G
    R E J O I C E

    S I N G I N G
    J O Y F U L L Y
G L A D N E S S
```

WE ARE THANKFUL p.27

T | THCLOES | C L O (T) H E S
H | RUCHCH | C (H) U R C H
A | MALSANI | (A) N I M A L S
N | SDNEIRF | F R I E (N) D S
K | KOOBS | B O O (K) S
Y | MAFLIY | F A M I L (Y)
O | MEHO | H (O) M E
U | SELFYOUR | Y O (U) R S E L F
G | DOG | (G) O D
O | TSOY | T (O) Y S
D | DOOF | F O O (D)

WHAT DID THEY BRING? p.34

DOLG G (O) L (D)

ESNECNIKNARF F (R) A N K I N S (E) N C E

RHRYM M Y R R (H)

Print the circled letters here. O D R E H

Unscramble them and print them in these spaces.

H E R O D

Who was this person?

HEROD SENT THE WISE MEN TO FIND JESUS

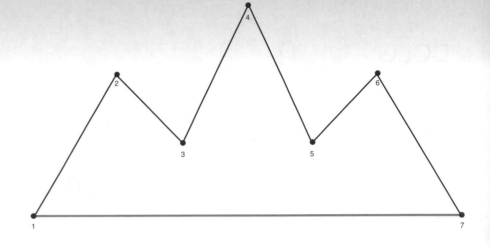

WHO IS JESUS? p.39

S	SUSEJ	J E (S) U S
A	RACES	C (A) R E S
V	OVEL	L O (V) E
I	ENDFRI	F R (I) E N D
O	IONNAPMOC	C O M P A N I (O) N
R	PERLEH	H E L P E (R)

WHAT'S THAT IN THE SKY? p.105

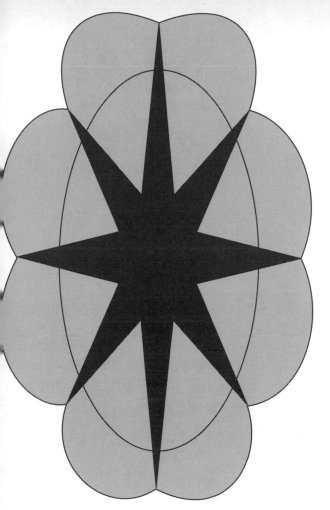

WHAT DID THEY RIDE? p.107

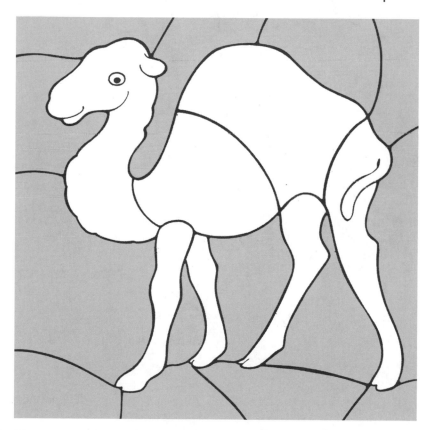

GOD THINKS I'M SPECIAL p.112

A=1; B=2; C=3; D=4; E=5; F=6; G=7; H=8; I=9; J=10; K=11; L=12;

M=13; N=14; O=15; P=16; Q=17; R=18; S=19; T-20; U=21; V=22;

W=23; X=24; Y=25; Z=26

G O D   M A D E   E   M E
7 15 4   13 1 4   5   13 5

S P E C I A L .
19 16 5 3 9 1 12

WHAT IS THIS? p.118

LEASTING   Ⓢ T E A L I N G

TEACHING   C H E A T Ⓘ N G

BNIEG NAEM   B E I N G   M E A Ⓝ

NESSRUDE   R U D E N E Ⓢ S

Print the circled letters here S I N S .

GETTING TO KNOW YOUR BIBLE p.127

__B__ __U__ __T__ those who wait for the LORD shall renew their strength, they shall mount up with wings like eagles, they shall run and not be weary, they shall walk and not faint. (Isaiah 40:31)

__T__ __H__ __E__ LORD is my shepherd, I shall not want. (Psalm 23:1)

Every __W__ __O__ __R__ __D__ of God proves true; he is a shield to those who take refuge in him. (Proverbs 30:5)

And she gave birth to her firstborn son, and wrapped him in bands __O__ __F__ cloth, and laid him in a manger, because there was no place for them at the inn. (Luke 2:7)

Blessed are __T__ __H__ __E__ pure in heart, for they will see God. (Matthew 5:8)

My help comes from the __L__ __O__ __R__ __D__ who made heaven and earth. (Psalm 121:2)

O give thanks to the LORD. . . for his steadfast love __E__ __N__ __D__ __U__ __R__ __E__ __S__ forever. (Psalm 136:1)

For the LORD is good; his steadfast love endures __F__ __O__ __R__ __E__ __V__ __E__ __R__, and his faithfulness to all generations. (Psalm 100:5)

Print each word you found in the spaces below. They spell out another Bible verse.

__B__ __U__ __T__   __T__ __H__ __E__   __W__ __O__ __R__ __D__   __O__ __F__   __T__ __H__ __E__   __L__ __O__ __R__ __D__

__E__ __N__ __D__ __U__ __R__ __E__ __S__   __F__ __O__ __R__ __E__ __V__ __E__ __R__.

__P__ __E__ __T__ __E__ R 1: __2__ __5__)

WHO IS SPECIAL? p.132

WHO IS SPECIAL? p.133

COME BE BAPTIZED p.142

p.142

OWN

Jesus was baptized in the **JORDAN** River. (Mark 1:9)

Baptism is a sign of **GOD'S** love for us.

We can baptize people when they are babies, children,

or **ADULTS** .

When Jesus was baptized, the Holy Spirit descended

upon him in the form of a dove. God said, "You are my

Son, the Beloved, with you I am **WELL** pleased."

Luke 3:22)

ROSS

John the Baptist baptized **JESUS** . (Matthew 3:13)

It is important for parents to **TEACH** their chil-

dren about God and Jesus.

When we baptize people we welcome them to God's

FAMILY .

Put the circled letters here. **ATERW**

Unscramble them to form

a word. **W A T E R**

What is important about this word?

WE BAPTIZE WITH WATER

BACK TO SCHOOL   p.145

Draw lines through each clue. Clues go down or across. Two clues go in two directions. They are FIELD TRIPS
and SOCIAL STUDIES . Which two clues are listed twice?   ART   and GYM   . When you are finished,
you will have several letters left over. Circle them with red pencil. What do they spell? PRINCIPAL

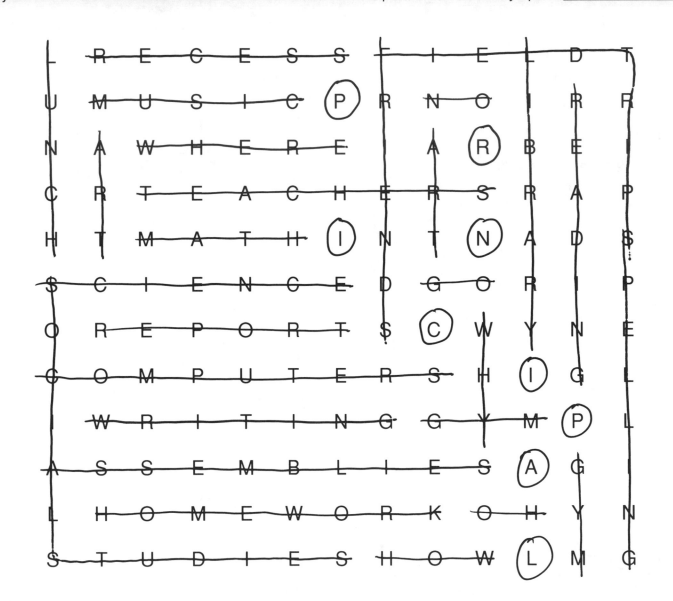

Teachers
Report
Reading
Computers
Math
Homework
Science
Library
Social Studies
Lunch
Gym
Friends
Art
Assemblies
Music
Where
Writing
Go
Recess
Oh
Field Trips
Why
Spelling
No
How

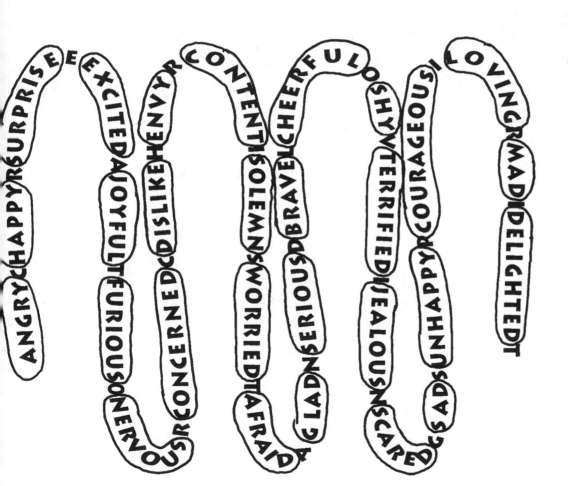

HOW DO I FEEL?   p.153

Angry
Scared
Surprise
Worried
Glad
Serious

Happy
Joyful
Sad
Terrified
Unhappy
Loving

Furious
Delighted
Concerned
Excited
Dislike
Mad

Jealous
Envy
Nervous
Afraid
Content

Shy
Brave
Courageous
Cheerful
Solemn

CREA(T)OR CH(R)(I)ST AND LOV(I)(N)G SP(I)R(I)(T).

The circled letters

spell T R I N I T y

WHAT ARE WE DOING? p.157

PRAY

SING

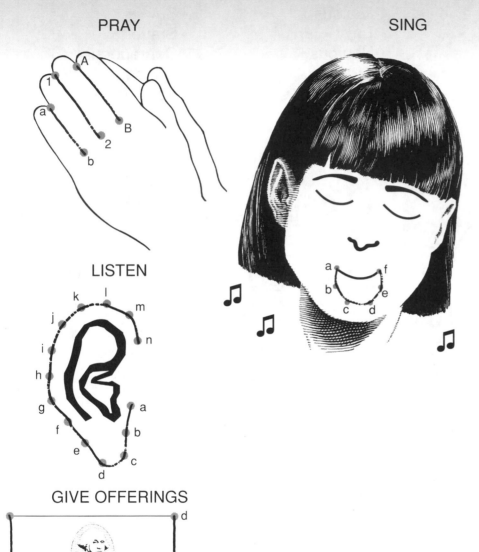

LISTEN

GIVE OFFERINGS

WHAT'S IN A WORSHIP SERVICE? p.157

1. CALL TO WORSHIP __8__ These are the gifts we offer to God.

2. INTROIT __9__ This closes the worship service.

3. PRAYERS __7__ This tells what we believe about God.

4. LITANY __6__ These are songs we sing in church.

5. SERMON __3__ These are the things we say to God. We use them to thank God and to ask God for help.

6. MUSIC __1__ This opens church. It is an invitation to worship God. It gets us "warmed up for church."

7. AFFIRMATION __4__ This is a series of thoughts about God. It has a responsive line.

8. OFFERINGS __2__ This is a musical invitation that opens church.

9. BENEDICTIONS __5__ This is a message that teaches us how to be good Christians.

HELP THE SHEPHERD FIND HIS LOST SHEEP p.48

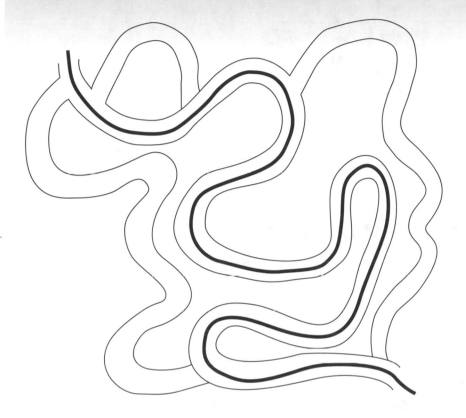

JESUS LOVES YOU p.51

LET'S FIND JESUS p.53

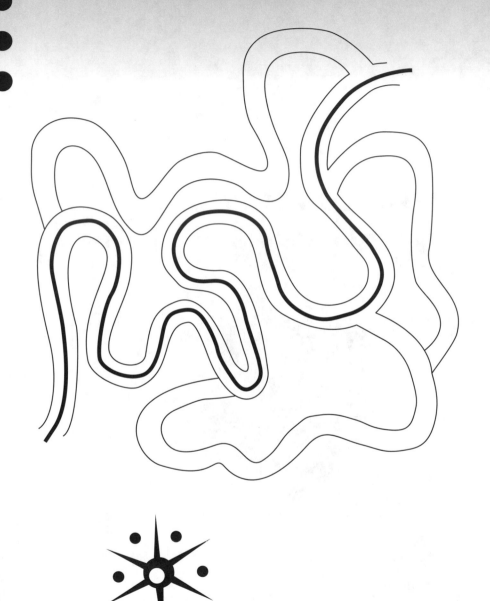

WHO DO YOU BELIEVE? p.56

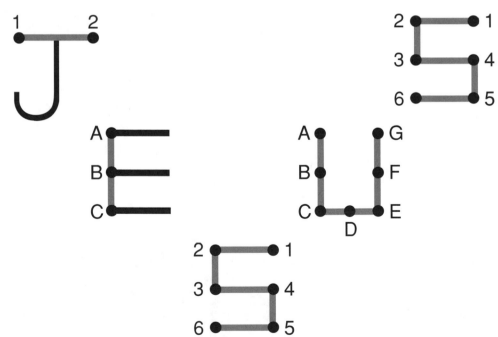

A SHAMROCK TRINITY

p.59

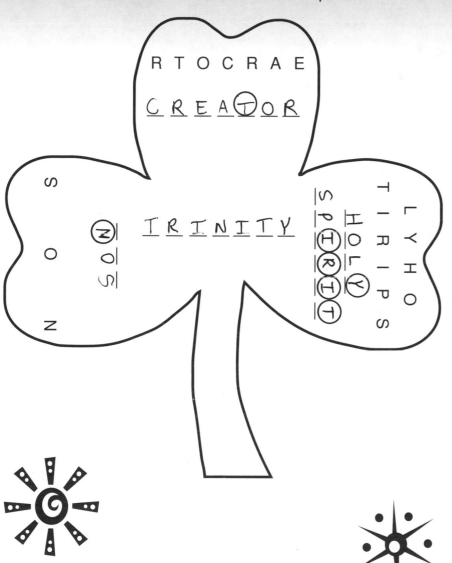

R T O C R A E

C R E A T O R

T R I N I T Y

S O N

S O N

L Y H O

T I R I P S

S P I R I T

H O L Y

WHAT DOES GOD WANT US TO DO?

p.65

PRAY

LET'S PRAY   p.67

1. We can ask God to (ELHP) H E L **P** us to do our best in school.

2. When we do something wrong, we can ask God to (GIVEFOR) F O **R** G I V E us.

3. When we are (FRAAID) A F R **A** I D we can ask God to help us.

4. God loves (OUY) **Y** O U .

5. We can ask God to stay (HITW) **W** I T H us wherever we go.

6. Remember, that Jesus came to be our (VIORSA) S A V **I** O R .

7. We should ask God to help our (CHTEARES) **T** E A C H E R S at (CHSOOL) S C **H** O O L .

8. We can ask God to give us (DOFO) F **O** O D .

9. Remember, God will stay with you during a scary (STORMTHUNDER) T H **U** N D E R S **T** O R M .

10. We can ask God to give us the (THCLOES) **C** L O T H E S we need to wear.

11. We can ask God to give us a (MOHE) H O M **E** .

12. Remember, God (WAYSAL) A L W **A** Y S loves us.

13. God likes to hear us (GNIS) **S** I N G prayers.

14. We should ask God to help us do what is (GHRIT) R **I** G H T .

15. God (DEENS) **N** E E D S all of us.

16. Remember that (DOG) **G** O D is your friend.

Write the circled letters in the spaces below.

P R A Y   W I T H O U T   C E A S I N G

(1 SALONTHESIANS) T H E S S A L O N I A N S 5:17   What does this verse mean?

WE SHOULD ALWAYS PRAY

WHAT SHOULD WE DO? p.71

J FULJOY Ⓙ O Y F U L

U CUHRCH C H Ⓤ R C H

S SEHTOLC C L O T H E Ⓢ

T CHATEERS Ⓣ E A C H E R S

A MAFILY F Ⓐ M I L Y

S COOLSH Ⓢ C H O O L

K THERO SKID O T H E R Ⓚ I D S

G NESSGIVEFOR F O R Ⓖ I V E N E S S

O TORASP P A S T Ⓞ R

D FODO F O O Ⓓ

WHAT CAN WE DO? p.80

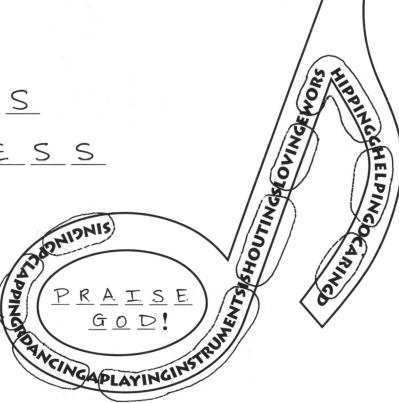

PRAISE GOD!

SINGING CLAPPING DANCING PLAYING INSTRUMENTS SHOUTING LOVING WORS HIPPING HELPING CARING

WHEN WE PRAY

p.81

WHAT ARE YOU SAYING?

p.94

THE LORD BLESS
20 8 5   12 15 17 4   2 12 15 19 19

YOU AND KEEP YOU
25 15 21   1 14 4   11 5 5 16   25 15 21

THE LORD MAKE HIS
20 8 5   12 15 18 4   13 1 11 5   8 9 19

FACE TO SHINE
6 1 3 5   20 15   19 8 9 14 5

UPON YOU AND BE
21 16 15 14   25 15 21   1 14 4   2 5

GRACIOUS TO YOU
7 18 1 3 9 15 21 19   20 15   25 15 21

THE LORD LIFT UP
20 8 5   12 15 18 4   12 9 6 20   21 16

HIS COUNTENANCE
8 9 19   3 15 21 14 20 5 14 1 14 3 5

UPON YOU AND GIVE
21 16 15 14   25 15 21   1 14 4   7 9 22 5

YOU PEACE.
25 15 21   16 5 1 3 5

NUMBERS 6:24-26
14 21 13 2 5 18 19

WE ARE BAPTIZED p.95

RCOETAR

C R E A T O R

ONS

SON

N I G V I L
R I T S I P
S P I R I T
L I V I N G

L
O
V
E

WHO ARE WE? p.97

TEREP	P	E	T	E	R					
MAJES	J	A	M	E	S					
NHOJ	J	O	H	N						
DREWAN	A	N	D	R	E	W				
LIPHIP	P	H	I	L	I	P				
MEWTHOOLRAB	B	A	R	T	H	O	L	O	M	E	W
HATMTEW	M	A	T	T	H	E	W			
MASTOH	T	H	O	M	A	S				
SEMJA	J	A	M	E	S					
SADEUTHD	T	H	A	D	D	E	U	S		
ISMNO	S	I	M	O	N					
ADJSU	J	U	D	A	S					

Print the circled letters here. P D I L S E I S

Print the squared letters here. A O P L E S T S

Unscramble both sets of letters to fill in the blanks.

These men were the D I S C I P L E S of Jesus Christ.

They were also called the twelve A P O S T L E S.

WHAT DID YOU SAY? p.99

WHAT AM I? p.101

HOW LONG? p.103